Power Maths

Year 4 Textbook

Series Editor: Tony Staneff

C000085100

Flo

Flo is flexible and creative. She often comes up with new methods.

curious

Ash

brave

Astrid

determined

helpful

Dexter

Sparks

Pearson

Contents

Unit 6 – Multiplication and division (2)   6

Problem solving – addition and multiplication   8

Problem solving – mixed problems   12

Using written methods to multiply   16

Multiplying a 2-digit number by a 1-digit number   20

Multiplying a 3-digit number by a 1-digit number   24

Problem solving – multiplication   28

Multiplying more than two numbers (1)   32

Multiplying more than two numbers (2)   36

Problem solving – mixed correspondence problems   40

Dividing a 2-digit number by a 1-digit number (1)   44

Division with remainders   48

Dividing a 2-digit number by a 1-digit number (2)   52

Dividing a 2-digit number by a 1-digit number (3)   56

Dividing a 3-digit number by a 1-digit number   60

Problem solving – division   64

End of unit check   68

Unit 7 – Measure – area   70

What is area?   72

Counting squares (1)   76

Counting squares (2)   80

Making shapes   84

Comparing area   88

End of unit check   92

This tells you which page you need.

Unit 8 – Fractions (1)   94
Tenths and hundredths (1)   96
Tenths and hundredths (2)   100
Equivalent fractions (1)   104
Equivalent fractions (2)   108
Simplifying fractions   112
Fractions greater than 1 (1)   116
Fractions greater than 1 (2)   120
End of unit check   124

Unit 9 – Fractions (2)   126
Adding fractions   128
Subtracting fractions (1)   132
Subtracting fractions (2)   136
Problem solving – adding and subtracting fractions (1)   140
Problem solving – adding and subtracting fractions (2)   144
Calculating fractions of a quantity   148
Problem solving – fraction of a quantity (1)   152
Problem solving – fraction of a quantity (2)   156
End of unit check   160

Unit 10 – Decimals (1)   162
Tenths (1)   164
Tenths (2)   168
Tenths (3)   172
Dividing by 10 (1)   176
Dividing by 10 (2)   180
Hundredths (1)   184
Hundredths (2)   188
Hundredths (3)   192
Dividing by 100   196
Dividing by 10 and 100   200
End of unit check   204

What have we learnt?   208

Are you ready for some more maths?

3

How to use this book

These pages make sure we're ready for the unit ahead. Find out what we'll be learning and brush up on your skills.

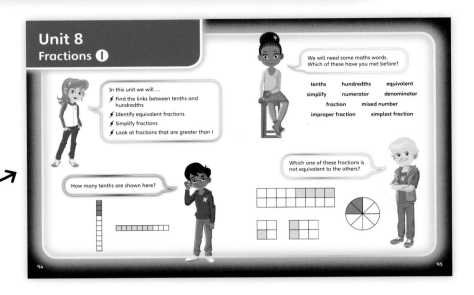

Discover

Lessons start with **Discover**.

Here, we explore new maths problems.

Can you work out how to find the answer?

Don't be afraid to make mistakes. Learn from them and try again!

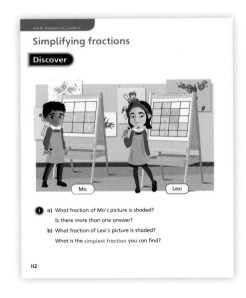

Share

Next, we share our ideas with the class.

Did we all solve the problems the same way?
What ideas can you try?

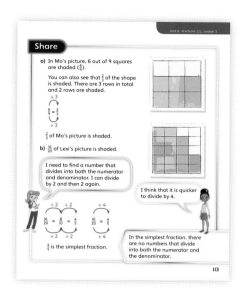

Think together

Then we have a go at some
more problems together.
Use what you have just
learnt to help you.

We'll try a challenge too!

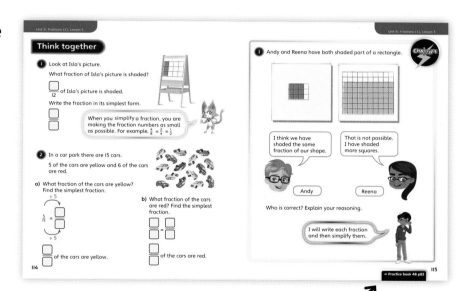

This tells you which
page to go to in your
Practice Book.

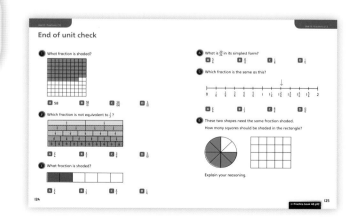

At the end of each unit there's an
End of unit check. This is our chance
to show how much we have learnt.

Unit 6
Multiplication and division ②

In this unit we will …

⚡ Learn how to multiply a number using the written method

⚡ Learn how to multiply and divide numbers in our heads

⚡ Find the remainder when a number is divided

⚡ Use bar models and part-whole models to solve multiplication and division problems

We have already learnt the times-tables facts. Can you use the facts to work out how many chocolates I have? Is there a quicker way?

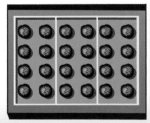 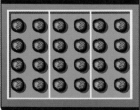

We will need some maths words. How many of these have you used before?

multiply   divide   times-tables

partition   array   bar model

part-whole model   remainder

factor pair   factors   commutative

We need to know how to use a part-whole model to multiply or divide. First, we need to know how to partition a number. Is there another way to partition 36?

36 = 30 + 6

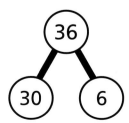

36 = 20 + 16

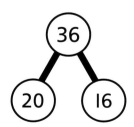

Problem solving – addition and multiplication

Discover

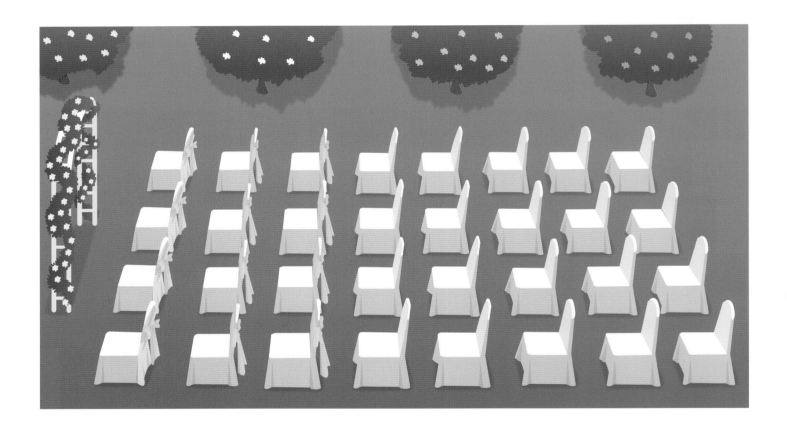

1 **a)** How many chairs have bows?

How many plain chairs are there?

b) How many chairs are there in total?

Find two ways of working out the total.

Share

a) There are 4 rows of 3 chairs with bows.
There are 4 rows of 5 plain chairs.

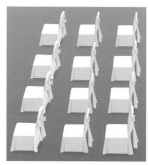
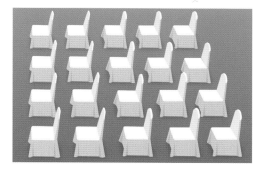

$4 \times 3 = 12$
12 chairs have bows.

$4 \times 5 = 20$
There are 20 plain chairs.

b)

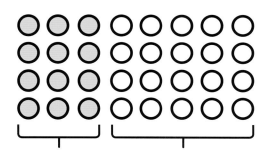
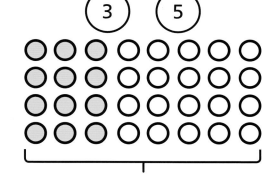

$4 \times 3 = 12$ $4 \times 5 = 20$ $4 \times 8 = 32$

$12 + 20 = 32$

I just added the numbers from earlier.

There are 32 chairs in total.

I did $3 + 5 = 8$, which gives the number of chairs in each row.

Then I multiplied my answer by 4, as there are 4 rows.

Think together

① How many chairs are there in total?

Find the answers using the two methods.

Method 1

Chairs with bows: $\boxed{}$ × 3 = $\boxed{}$

Plain chairs: $\boxed{}$ × 3 = $\boxed{}$

$\boxed{}$ + $\boxed{}$ = $\boxed{}$

Method 2

$\boxed{}$ + $\boxed{}$ = $\boxed{}$

3 × $\boxed{}$ = $\boxed{}$

There are $\boxed{}$ chairs in total.

② Work out the total number of cupcakes.

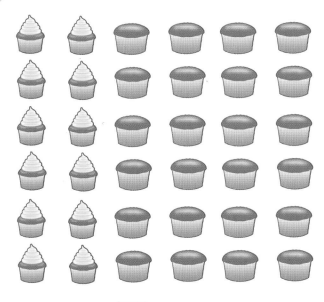

There are $\boxed{}$ cupcakes in total.

3 **a)** Use the counters to help you to work out:
2 × 5 + 2 × 7

CHALLENGE

Explain your method to your partner.

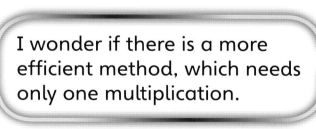

I found the number of counters in each group and then added these together.

I wonder if there is a more efficient method, which needs only one multiplication.

b) Show that 7 × 3 + 7 × 2 = 7 × 5

c) Show that 2 × 4 + 3 × 2 = 7 × 2

11

Problem solving – mixed problems

Discover

1 a) How many butterflies are there in the tray?

   b) The butterflies are put into new trays.

   Each tray holds 12 butterflies.

   How many new trays are needed?

Share

a) There are 6 rows of 8 butterflies.

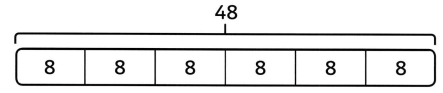

$6 \times 8 = 48$

There are 48 butterflies in the tray.

I used my knowledge of arrays, and then the facts from the 8 times-table, to work this out.

b) There are 48 butterflies. Each tray holds 12 butterflies.

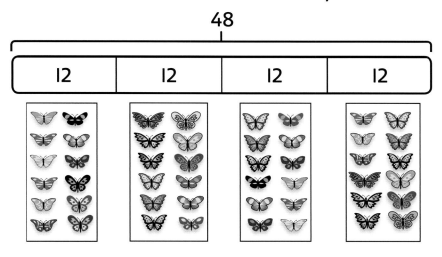

$48 \div 12 = 4$

4 new trays are needed.

I grouped the butterflies into 12s. This showed it was a division.

13

Think together

1 There are 8 pencils in each box.

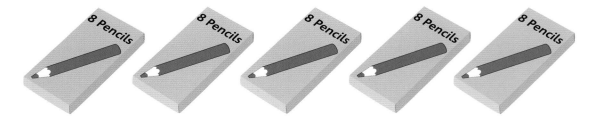

a) How many pencils are there in total?

☐ × ☐ = ☐

There are ☐ pencils in total.

b) The pencils are shared between 2 classes.

How many pencils does each class get?

☐ ÷ ☐ = ☐

Each class gets ☐ pencils.

2 Work out the missing value.

6	6	6	6

?	?	?

? = ☐

 3 There are 5 toy cars. They cost the same, in total, as 3 toy planes.

How much does a toy plane cost?

A toy plane costs £ ⬚ .

I will draw bar models to help me to work out the missing number.

Let's put one bar model above the other. Do they need to be the same length?

→ **Practice book 4B p9**

Using written methods to multiply

Discover

There are 10 trees in this orchard. Each tree has 6 apples on it.

Andy

There are 8 trees in this orchard. Each tree has 6 apples on it.

Jamilla

1 **a)** How many apples does each orchard have?

b) How many apples are there in total?

Share

a) There are 10 trees in Andy's orchard and 8 trees in Jamilla's orchard.

Each tree has 6 apples.

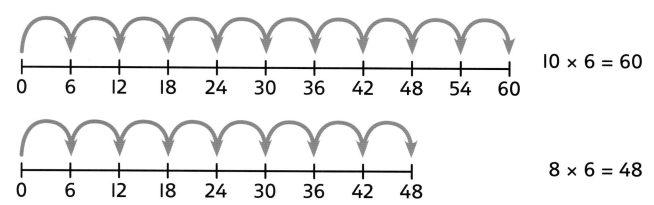

$10 \times 6 = 60$

$8 \times 6 = 48$

Andy's orchard has 60 apples. Jamilla's orchard has 48 apples.

b) $60 + 48 = 108$

There are 108 apples in total.

> I added the two answers together.

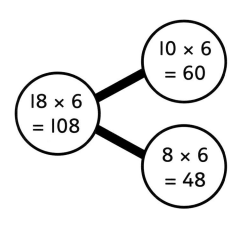

$18 \times 6 = 10 \times 6 + 8 \times 6$

$= 60 + 48$

$= 108$

> I did 18×6 to find the total. There are 18 trees in total and 6 apples in each tree.

There are 108 apples in total.

Think together

1 Lexi and Jamilla have some bags of pears. Each bag contains 5 pears.

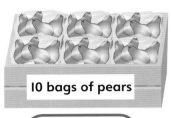

10 bags of pears

Lexi

6 bags of pears

Jamilla

How many pears do they have in total?

Lexi: $\boxed{} \times 5 = \boxed{}$ Jamilla: $\boxed{} \times 5 = \boxed{}$

$\boxed{} + \boxed{} = \boxed{}$

They have $\boxed{}$ pears in total.

2 Oranges come in bags of 6.

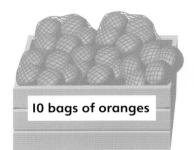

10 bags of oranges

4 bags of oranges

a) How many oranges are in total?

$\boxed{} \times \boxed{} = \boxed{}$ $\boxed{} \times \boxed{} = \boxed{}$

There are $\boxed{}$ oranges in 10 bags.

There are $\boxed{}$ oranges in 4 bags.

$\boxed{} + \boxed{} = \boxed{}$

There are $\boxed{}$ oranges in total.

b) What single calculation could you have done instead to find the answer?

$\boxed{} \times 6 = \boxed{}$

18

3 Here are some counters.

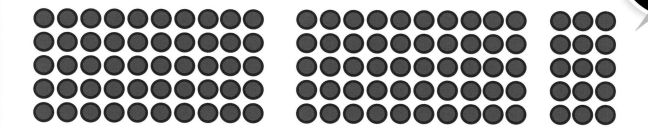

CHALLENGE

Richard and Kate are trying to work out the total number of counters.

I did 5 × 10, 5 × 10 and 5 × 3 and added them together.

I did 5 × 20 and then 5 × 3 and added them together.

Richard

Kate

a) Explain the methods that Richard and Kate have used.

b) Is it possible to work out the answer using just one multiplication? If so, how can you do this?

I will draw with my finger around the different groups to help me.

19

Multiplying a 2-digit number by a 1-digit number

Discover

1 **a)** Danny and Bella have used different methods to work out 23 × 5.

What is the same and what is different about the two methods?

b) Use place value counters to show what Danny has done.

Share

a) Both methods use columns. Both methods give the same answer. Bella has used long (expanded) multiplication, but Danny has used short (single line) multiplication.

I think Danny has gone wrong. He has missed a step!

No, I can see what he has done. He has just done it all in one line. It is quicker that way.

b) This shows the calculation 23 × 5.

There are 5 rows with 23 in each row.

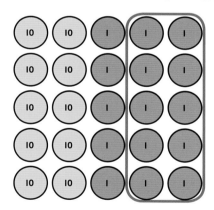 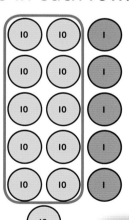 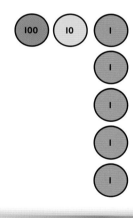

```
    2  3
×      5
─────────
  1  1  5
      ①
```

The I under the line represents the extra 10 that is made when an exchange is done.

II tens and 5 ones = I hundred, I ten and 5 ones

So, 23 × 5 = II5

21

Think together

1 Use place value counters to show the answer to 22 × 6.

Write down the calculation you are doing, as you move the counters.

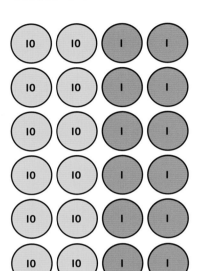

$$22 \times 6 = \boxed{}$$

```
      2   2
  ×       6
  _____

  _____
```

2 **a)** Work out 26 × 5.

```
      2   6
  ×       5
  _____

  _____
```

$$26 \times 5 = \boxed{}$$

b) What is different about the working out for this question?

a) Work out the missing numbers.

$32 \times 4 = \boxed{}$

$23 \times 6 = \boxed{}$

$43 \times 7 = \boxed{}$

$38 \times 4 = \boxed{}$

I can see a pattern in my working out …

b) What do you notice about the exchanges each time?

c) Work out a fifth question to continue the pattern.

I am going to use my times-tables facts to help me to find the missing numbers.

 CHALLENGE

23

Multiplying a 3-digit number by a 1-digit number

Discover

Row A:
Seats 1–52

1 **a)** There are 6 rows of seats in each section. Each row has 52 seats.

How many seats are there in a section?

b) There are 3 sections in the stadium.

How many seats are there in total?

Share

a) There are 6 rows of seats in each section.

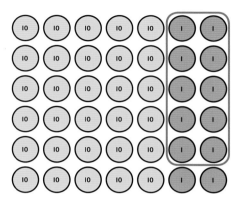
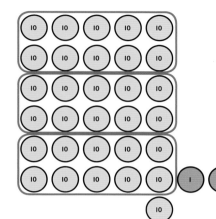
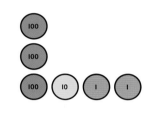

$$\begin{array}{r} 5\ 2 \\ \times \quad 6 \\ \hline 3\ 1\ 2 \\ \end{array}$$

I wonder if I could use this method to multiply a 3-digit number by a 1-digit number.

$6 \times 52 = 312$

There are 312 seats in a section.

b) There are 3 sections in the stadium. Each section contains 312 seats.

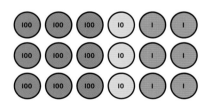

$$\begin{array}{r} 3\ 1\ 2 \\ \times \quad\ \ 3 \\ \hline 9\ 3\ 6 \\ \end{array}$$

$312 \times 3 = 936$

There are 936 seats in total.

Think together

1 There are 146 sweets in a jar.

How many sweets are there in 2 jars?

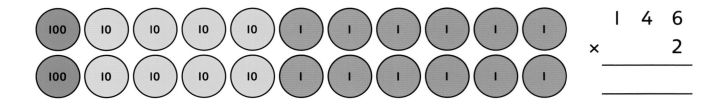

$$
\begin{array}{r}
1\ 4\ 6 \\
\times\ 2 \\
\hline
 \\
\end{array}
$$

There are ☐ sweets in 2 jars.

2 A plane holds 136 passengers.

How many passengers are there in 4 full planes?

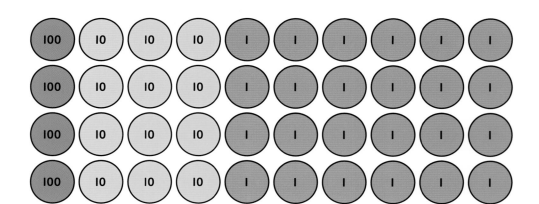

$$
\times\ \underline{}
$$

There are ☐ passengers in 4 planes.

③

| 1 | 2 | 3 |

Arrange the number cards to make these answers.

| 738 | | 1,386 | | 1,872 |

$$
\begin{array}{r}
\times \quad 6 \\
\hline
7 \quad 3 \quad 8 \\
\end{array}
\qquad
\begin{array}{r}
\times \quad 6 \\
\hline
1 \quad 3 \quad 8 \quad 6 \\
\end{array}
\qquad
\begin{array}{r}
\times \quad 6 \\
\hline
1 \quad 8 \quad 7 \quad 2 \\
\end{array}
$$

I looked at the last digit of each number to help me to work out the answers.

Use your knowledge of times-tables to help you.

27

Problem solving – multiplication

Discover

1 **a)** How many people are going to Bolton Towers?

b) How many people are going on a trip today?

Share

a) There are 56 people on each coach going to Bolton Towers.

There are 3 coaches.

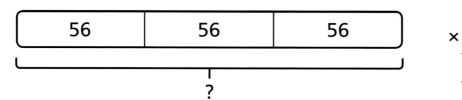

56	56	56

?

```
    5  6
×      3
─────────
  1  6  8
       1
```

There are 168 people going to Bolton Towers.

b) We know that 168 people are going to Bolton Towers.

?

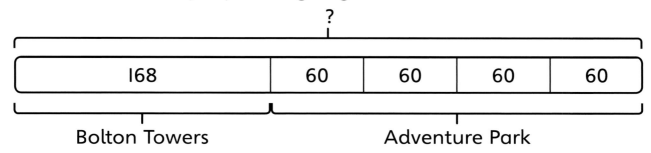

168	60	60	60	60

Bolton Towers   Adventure Park

> To work out the total I did
> 56 + 56 + 56 + 60 + 60 + 60 + 60.

There are 4 coaches going to Adventure Park.

There are 60 people on each coach.

$60 × 4 = 240$

There are 240 people going to Adventure Park.

$168 + 240 = 408$

There are 408 people going on a trip today.

> I used the answer from earlier and then
> used 6 × 4 to help me to do 60 × 4.
>
> Then I added my answers together.

29

Think together

1 In another school, there are 9 coaches going on a trip.

There are 4 coaches going to Bolton Towers. There are 5 coaches going to Adventure Park.

Bolton Towers   Adventure Park

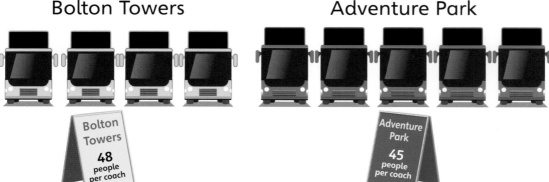

Bolton Towers
48 people per coach

Adventure Park
45 people per coach

How many people in total are going on a trip?

◻ × 4 = ◻

◻ people are going to Bolton Towers.

◻ × 5 = ◻

◻ people are going to Adventure Park.

◻ + ◻ = ◻

There are ◻ people in total going on a trip.

2 On a school trip, 117 children are going ice skating and 136 children are going bowling.

What is the difference between the total cost of the bowling trip and the ice skating trip?

ICE SKATING
£9 PER CHILD

BOWLING
£7 PER CHILD

3 A theatre has 385 tickets available for a play.

Tickets cost £6 each.

A school wants to send 7 coaches with 48 people on each coach.

a) How many tickets will be available after the school has bought all of the tickets they need?

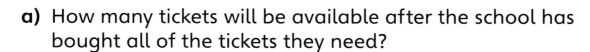
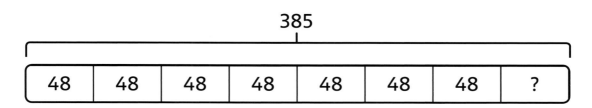

385

| 48 | 48 | 48 | 48 | 48 | 48 | 48 | ? |

b) What is the total cost of sending everyone to see the play?

I wonder if I just multiply 385 by 6.

I think I may need to use a number from part a) to answer this question.

31

Multiplying more than two numbers ①

Discover

① **a)** How many stickers are there on 1 sheet?

    b) How many stickers are there, in total, on the teacher's desk?

Share

a) There are 5 rows of 2 stickers.

$2 + 2 + 2 + 2 + 2 = 10$

Or, $2 \times 5 = 10$

There are 10 stickers on 1 sheet.

b)

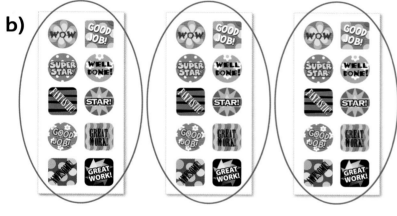

I worked out how many stickers there are on each sheet and multiplied by 3.

$5 \times 2 \times 3 = 30$

$10 \times 3 = 30$

I counted how many are in each column. There are 2 columns. The answer is the same!

There are 30 stickers, in total, on the teacher's desk.

Think together

1 How many stickers are there on 6 sheets?

5 × 2 × 6 = ☐   or   2 × 5 × 6 = ☐

☐ × 6 = ☐   ☐ × 6 = ☐

There are ☐ stickers on 6 sheets.

2 A box contains 3 rows of 6 doughnuts.

a) How many doughnuts are there in 2 boxes?

☐ × ☐ × ☐ = ☐

There are ☐ doughnuts in 2 boxes.

b) How many doughnuts are there in 5 boxes?

There are ☐ doughnuts in 5 boxes.

You could draw a diagram to help you.

3 Luis and Isla are working out the answer to this question:

CHALLENGE

$9 \times 2 \times 5$

I did $9 \times 2 = 18$ and then $18 \times 5 = 90$.

I did $2 \times 5 = 10$ and then multiplied my answer by 9. $10 \times 9 = 90$

Luis

Isla

a) Which method do you think is more efficient? Why?

b) What is the most efficient method to use to work out the following:

$2 \times 7 \times 6$

$3 \times 4 \times 5$

$9 \times 8 \times 2$

I can multiply the numbers in any order and still get the same answer.

This means that multiplication is **commutative**. Using a different order can help you to multiply mentally.

35

→ Practice book 4B p24

Multiplying more than two numbers ❷

Discover

1 **a)** Find all the pairs of numbers that multiply together to make 24.

b) How can Richard use these numbers to help him to work out 24 × 5?

Share

a)

A factor is a number that divides by another number equally.

A factor pair is two numbers that multiply together to make the number.

I started from 1 ×, then 2 × and went one number at a time, until the numbers started repeating.

1 × 24

2 × 12

3 × 8

4 × 6

b) Richard can use the numbers from part a) to help him to find the numbers that are easiest to multiply together.

Remember, we can multiply numbers in any order and get the same answer.

$24 = 2 \times 12$

So, 24×5 is equal to $2 \times 12 \times 5$

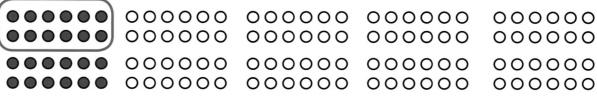

$12 \times 2 \times 5 =$

$12 \times 10 = 120$

So, $24 \times 5 = 120$

Think together

1 Richard is working out 55 × 6.

55 = 11 × 5

55 × 6 is equal to 11 × 5 × 6

Richard

a) What two numbers should Richard multiply together first?

☐ × ☐ = ☐

b) What two numbers should Richard then multiply to get the answer?

☐ × ☐ = ☐

2 Help Richard to work out these multiplications in his head.

a) 36 × 5

b) 18 × 18

I wonder if it would help if I separated 36 into 4 numbers.

I will think of each 18 as being 9 × 2.

3 Look at Richard's method for working out 6 × 48.

CHALLENGE

> 48 = 2 × 24
> 6 × 2 × 24 = 12 × 24

> I also know that 24 = 12 × 2
> So 12 × 24 is equal to 12 × 12 × 2

> I know that 12 × 12 = 144
> So 44 × 2 = 288

Richard

a) Is Richard correct?

b) What other methods could Richard have used to work out the answer?

> I am going to try to find different numbers that multiply to make 48.

> I need to write down some calculations. I wonder if I can do some in my head.

39

→ **Practice book 4B p27**

Problem solving – mixed correspondence problems

Discover

I **a)** Amelia wants to choose one bucket and one spade. How many different ways can she do this?

b) How does this link to the multiplication 5 × 4?

Share

a)

I will draw a line from each bucket to each spade and count the lines.

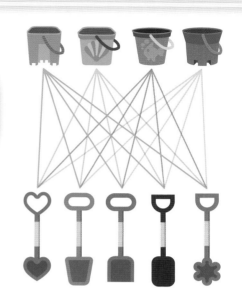

There are **20** different ways for Amelia to choose one bucket and one spade.

b)

	Bucket 1	Bucket 2	Bucket 3	Bucket 4
Spade 1				
Spade 2				
Spade 3				
Spade 4				
Spade 5				

This links to the multiplication 5 × 4 because there are 5 rows of 4 different matches.

This is 5 lots of 4.

5 × 4 = 20

I can see 5 rows of 4.

Each spade has 4 possible buckets. I did 4 + 4 + 4 + 4 + 4.

Think together

1 How many different ways could you choose one bucket and one spade?

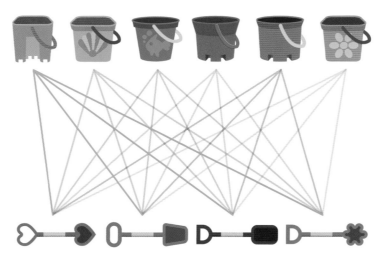

☐ × ☐ = ☐

There are ☐ different ways to choose one bucket and one spade.

2 Zac chooses one T-shirt and one pair of shorts to wear.

There are 30 different ways that Zac could choose what to wear.

How many pairs of shorts does he have?

6 × ☐ = 30

Zac has ☐ pairs of shorts.

42

③

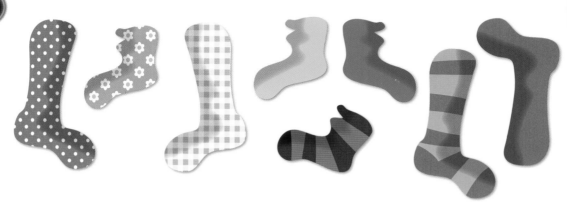

a) Choose two socks to make a mis-matched pair. How many different unique pairs could you choose?

I need to find out how many ways the socks can match up. I will make a grid.

Be careful not to count the same pair twice!

b) Find a quicker way to work out how many pairs of socks you can make.

I wonder if multiplication could help me.

→ Practice book 4B p30

Dividing a 2-digit number by a 1-digit number ❶

Discover

❶ a) 3 pieces of pineapple can fit on to each stick.

How many full sticks can be made?

b) The grapes are shared equally between 4 sticks.

How many grapes will be on each stick?

Share

a) There are 39 pieces of pineapple. Each stick can hold 3 pieces of pineapple.

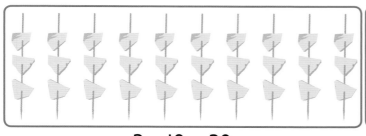 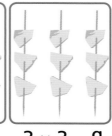 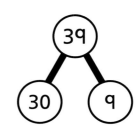

$3 \times 10 = 30$ $3 \times 3 = 9$

30 pieces of pineapple ÷ 3 = 10 sticks

9 pieces of pineapple ÷ 3 = 3 sticks

39 pieces of pineapple ÷ 3 = 13 sticks

13 full sticks can be made.

b) 48 grapes are shared equally between 4 sticks.

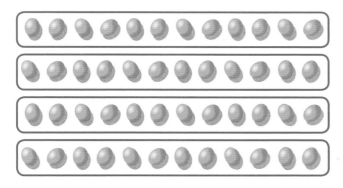

I did 48 ÷ 2 = 24 and then 24 ÷ 2 = 12, because I know that dividing by 4 is the same as halving twice.

48 can be split into 4 equal groups.

48 ÷ 4 = 12

Each group contains 12 grapes.

There will be 12 grapes on each stick.

Remember that 4 ÷ 4 = 1, so 40 ÷ 4 = 10.

Think together

1 There are 69 strawberries. If 3 strawberries fit on to one stick, how many full sticks can be made?

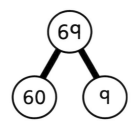

60 strawberries ÷ ⬚ = ⬚ full sticks

9 strawberries ÷ ⬚ = ⬚ full sticks

⬚ full sticks can be made using 69 strawberries.

2 There are 55 limes.

They are shared equally into 5 boxes.

How many limes are there in each box?

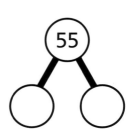

55 ÷ 5 = ⬚

a) Reena is trying to solve 68 ÷ 2. Check if her answer is correct.

CHALLENGE

10 lots of 2 is 20. I am going to see how many 20s fit into 68 and then divide what is left over.

I know that 30 lots of 2 is 60, and 4 lots of 2 is 8. So I worked out the answer to be 34 lots of 2.

Reena

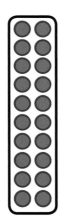  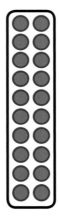

10 × 2 = 20   10 × 2 = 20   10 × 2 = 20   4 × 2 = 8

I think it is easier to divide 60 by 2 and then divide 8 by 2.

b) Use Reena's method to solve:

44 ÷ 2	84 ÷ 2	104 ÷ 2

→ Practice book 4B p33

Division with remainders

Discover

1 a) Work out 39 ÷ 3.

Does this calculation have a remainder?

b) Which two calculations on the whiteboard have a remainder?

Share

a) Divide the 10s into 3 groups. Divide the 1s into 3 groups.

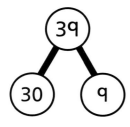

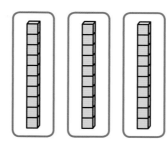

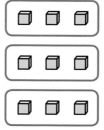

3 groups of 1 ten   3 groups of 3 ones

3 tens ÷ 3 = 3 groups of 1 ten   30 ÷ 3 = 10
9 ones ÷ 3 = 3 groups of 3 ones   9 ÷ 3 = 3
                                    10 + 3 = 13

This calculation does not have a remainder as it divides equally.

b) 85 ÷ 4 has a remainder.

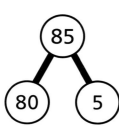

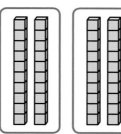

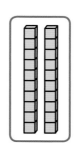

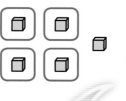

8 tens ÷ 4 = 2 tens   80 ÷ 4 = 20
5 ones ÷ 4 = 1 one, remainder 1   5 ÷ 4 = 1 r 1
85 ÷ 4 = 21 r 1

To divide 85 by 4, I used my knowledge that 80 ÷ 4 = 20.

57 ÷ 5 has a remainder.
5 tens ÷ 5 = 10 fives   50 ÷ 5 = 10
7 ones ÷ 5 = 1 one, remainder 2   7 ÷ 5 = 1 r 2
57 ÷ 5 = 11 r 2

I then divided the 1s and realised that there is 1 left over.

So, the two calculations with a remainder are 85 ÷ 4 and 57 ÷ 5.

Think together

1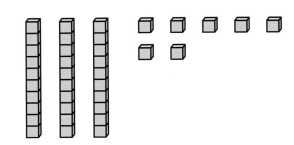

Find the missing numbers to work out $37 \div 3$.

Use the part-whole model to help you.

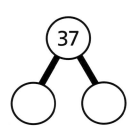

$\boxed{} \div 3 = \boxed{}$

$\boxed{} \div 3 = \boxed{}\ r\ \boxed{}$

So, $37 \div 3 = \boxed{}\ r\ \boxed{}$

Use 100s, 10s and 1s base 10 equipment to help you.

2 Show that $86 \div 4 = 21\ r\ 2$.

Fill in the missing numbers.

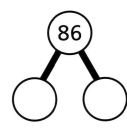

$\boxed{} \div 4 = \boxed{}$

$\boxed{} \div 4 = \boxed{}\ r\ \boxed{}$

So, $86 \div 4 = \boxed{}\ r\ \boxed{}$

3 The teacher has created four additional calculations.

$\boxed{} \div 3$

$4\boxed{} \div 4$

$67 \div \boxed{}$

$89 \div \boxed{}$

All four calculations have a remainder.

I think the answer to the first calculation could be 64 ÷ 3.

Amelia

a) Is Amelia correct?

Explain your answer.

b) What could the answer to each calculation be?

Remember to use 100s, 10s and 1s base 10 equipment, or place value counters to help you.

I wonder if sometimes it would help to partition a number into more than two parts. For example, I could partition 64 into 30 + 30 + 4.

64
30 30 4

→ **Practice book 4B p36**

Dividing a 2-digit number by a 1-digit number ②

Discover

Contains 56 bean bags

1 **a)** 56 bean bags have been used. There is an equal number of bean bags in each lane. How many bean bags are in each lane?

b) There is a bean bag every 10 metres in each lane.
How far is the furthest bean bag away from the start line?

Share

a) There are 56 bean bags altogether.

There are 4 running lanes.

$56 \div 4 = ?$

 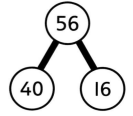

$40 \div 4 = 10$ $16 \div 4 = 4$

So, $56 \div 4 = 14$

There are 14 bean bags in each lane.

b) The first bean bag is 10 metres away from the start line.
The bean bags are then 10 metres apart.

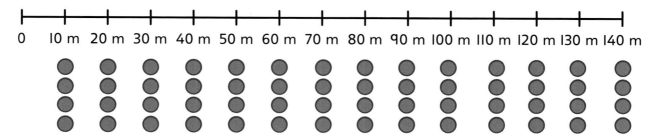

There are 14 bean bags in each lane.

There is one bean bag every 10 metres.

$14 \times 10 = 140$

The furthest bean bag is 140 metres away from the start line.

I thought the answer was 130 metres. I put the first bean bag at the start.

53

Think together

1 78 cones are divided equally across 6 lanes.

How many cones are in each lane?

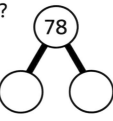

$\boxed{} \div 6 = \boxed{}$ $\boxed{} \div 6 = \boxed{}$

So, 78 ÷ 6 = $\boxed{}$

There are $\boxed{}$ cones in each lane.

I wonder if I could partition 78 in more than one way.

2 There are 76 children at the junior sports day.

There are 4 teams.

Each team has the same number of children.

How many children are in each team?

$\boxed{} \div \boxed{} = \boxed{}$

3 Zac is decorating cakes.

He has 72 cherries.

He puts 3 cherries on top of each cake and uses all the cherries.

He then packs all of the cakes into boxes of 4.

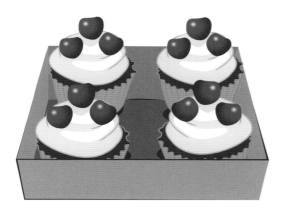

How many boxes of cakes does he pack?

I think I need to do more than one division. I will do one at a time though.

I think I can just divide by one number.

CHALLENGE

55

Dividing a 2-digit number by a 1-digit number ❸

Discover

1 **a)** What calculation has Lee done to get the answer 12?

b) What mistake has Lee made? What should the answer be?

Share

a) There are 7 days in a week.

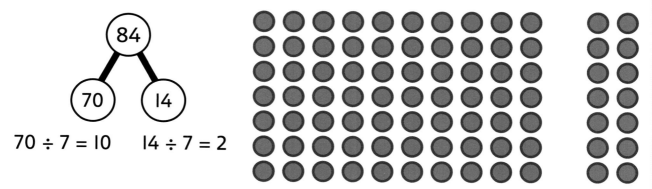

$70 \div 7 = 10 \qquad 14 \div 7 = 2$

$84 \div 7 = 12$

Lee has divided 84 by 7.

b) Lee has used full weeks, not school weeks.

There are only 5 days in a school week.

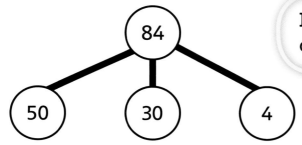

$50 \div 5 = 10 \qquad 30 \div 5 = 6$

I do not think 84 can be divided by 5.

I think it can, but it will have a remainder.

$84 \div 5 = 16$ remainder 4

The answer should be: they have 16 full school weeks and 4 days left.

57

Think together

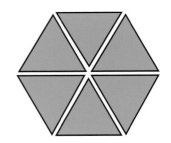

1 Ambika has 68 triangles. She puts them into groups of 6, to make hexagons.

a) How many hexagons can she make?

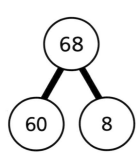

$60 \div 6 = \boxed{}$

$8 \div 6 = \boxed{}$ remainder $\boxed{}$

$68 \div 6 = \boxed{}$ remainder $\boxed{}$

Ambika can make $\boxed{}$ hexagons.

b) How many triangles will Ambika have left over?

She will have $\boxed{}$ triangles left over.

2 Use the part-whole model to help you to work out $79 \div 3$.

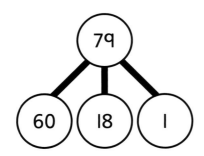

$\boxed{} \div \boxed{} = \boxed{} \ r \ \boxed{}$

58

3 Olivia and Lexi are working out 95 ÷ 4.

They each use a different part-whole model.

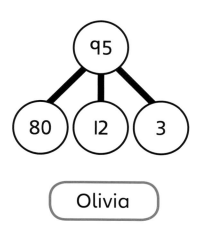

Olivia

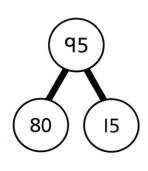

Lexi

a) Work out the answer to 95 ÷ 4 using both methods.

b) Which part-whole model do you prefer? Why?

These methods are nearly the same.

I wonder if you could partition 95 in other ways.

59

→ Practice book 4B p42

Dividing a 3-digit number by a 1-digit number

Discover

Each sheep needs 3 squares to graze on.

1 **a)** How many sheep can graze in the farmer's field?

b) A cow needs 4 squares to graze on.

How many cows can graze in the field?

Share

a) 11 × 12 = 132

There are 132 squares in total.

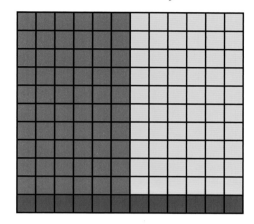

20 + 20 + 4 = 44

44 sheep can graze in the farmer's field.

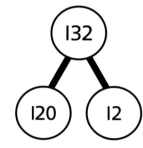

132

60   60   12

60 ÷ 3 = 20   60 ÷ 3 = 20   12 ÷ 3 = 4

132 ÷ 3 = 44

132

120   12

120 ÷ 3 = 40   12 ÷ 3 = 4

132

30   30   30   30   12

30 ÷ 3 = 10   30 ÷ 3 = 10   30 ÷ 3 = 10   30 ÷ 3 = 10   12 ÷ 3 = 4

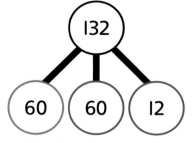

I partitioned the number of squares in different ways. I got the same answer each time.

b)

132

80   40   12

80 ÷ 4 = 20   40 ÷ 4 = 10   12 ÷ 4 = 3

132 ÷ 4 = 33

33 cows can graze in the field.

Think together

1 Find the answer to 146 ÷ 2.

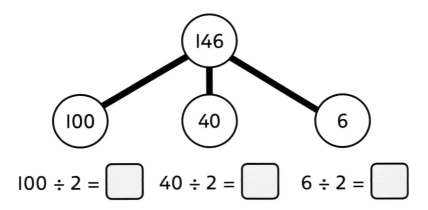

100 ÷ 2 = ☐   40 ÷ 2 = ☐   6 ÷ 2 = ☐

☐ + ☐ + ☐ = ☐

146 ÷ 2 = ☐

2 Use the part-whole model to find the answer to 185 ÷ 5.

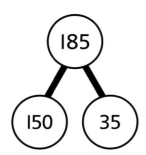

3 Here are three different ways of partitioning 168 ÷ 6.

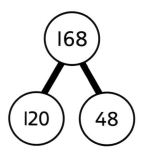
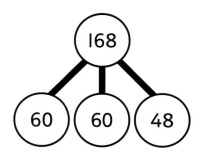
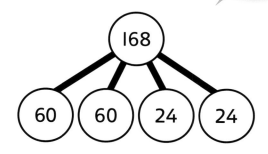

a) Choose a partition and use it to work out 168 ÷ 6.

b) Find three different ways of partitioning 246.

c) Use one of your partitions to work out 246 ÷ 3.

It does not matter which partition I use to help me divide. I will get the same answer.

I will try to solve this with just two parts!

→ **Practice book 4B p45**

Problem solving – division

Discover

1 a) How does Mo know that they cannot get into groups of 5?

How many children would be left over?

b) What group sizes could the children stand in without any being left over?

Share

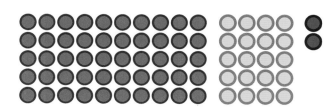

A number that divides equally by 5 must end in a 0 or 5.

a) There are 72 children.

Mo knows that 72 cannot be shared equally into 5 groups because 72 is not in the 5 times-table.

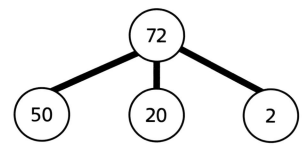

50 ÷ 5 = 10   20 ÷ 5 = 4

So, 72 ÷ 5 = 14 r 2

2 children would be left over.

b)

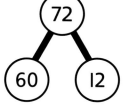 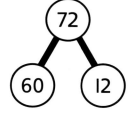 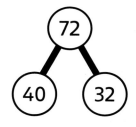 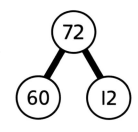

72 ÷ 2 = 36   72 ÷ 3 = 24   72 ÷ 4 = 18   72 ÷ 6 = 12

I made an array to show that 72 could be put into groups of 8 columns or 9 rows. This is because 9 × 8 = 72.

The children could stand in groups of 2, 3, 4, 6, 8, 9 and 12 without any being left over.

Think together

1 Children stand in groups of 3 or 4.

There are 59 children in total.

There are 5 groups of 4 children.

a) How many children are standing in groups of 4?

◻ × ◻ = ◻

There are ◻ children in groups of 4.

b) How many groups of 3 children are there?

◻ − ◻ = ◻

◻ ÷ ◻ = ◻

There are ◻ groups of 3 children

2 a) Find the answer to 73 ÷ 4.

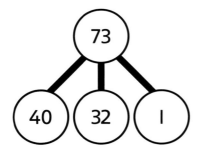

b) The answer to a question is 8 r 2. What could the question be?

3 Jamie is making a mosaic in art.

She has a piece of paper 60 cm by 60 cm.

She covers the piece of paper with rows, using strips of coloured paper that are 4 cm by 3 cm.

CHALLENGE

Jamie

How many pieces of coloured paper are needed to complete the mosaic?

I wonder how many pieces of paper there will be in each row.

I will try to make the same mosaic as a diagram on my desk. It will help me to work out what to do.

67

End of unit check

1 What is the last digit in the answer to 37 × 3?

A 0   B 1   C 3   D 10

2 How many boats cost the same as 9 snorkels?

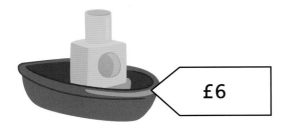
£6

£4

A 4   B 6   C 9   D 12

3 What digit should replace ★?

```
    3 3
  ×   5
  ─────
  1 ★ 5
```

A 0   B 1   C 6   D 8

4 Find the answer to this calculation.

$5 \times 7 \times 9 \times 2$

A 23 **B** 35 **C** 315 **D** 630

5 Which part-whole model does not help you to work out 78 ÷ 3?

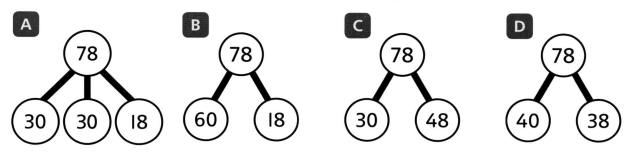

A 78 → 30, 30, 18   **B** 78 → 60, 18   **C** 78 → 30, 48   **D** 78 → 40, 38

6 Eggs are packed into boxes of 6 and 8.

The table below shows the number of each box sold.

Number of eggs in a box	Number of boxes sold
6	38
8	29

How many eggs were sold in total?

→ Practice book 4B p51

Unit 7
Measure – area

In this unit we will …

⚡ Learn what 'area' means

⚡ Find areas of shapes by counting squares

⚡ Draw shapes with different areas

⚡ Compare the area of different shapes

How many small squares fit into this large square?

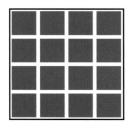

We will need some maths words. Which of these are new?

length   width   area   space

rectangle   square

rectilinear shape   unit   least

greatest   triangle   quadrilateral

reflection   rotation

Which shape do you think is larger? Why?

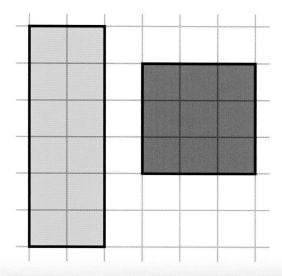

What is area?

Discover

1 **a)** Look at the picture. Which shape is larger, the door or the window? How do you know?

   b) Is there more than one way to find the answer?

Share

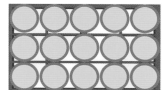

The **area** of a shape is the name we give to the space it takes up.

The larger the shape, the larger its area.

a)

$3 \times 5 = 15$

The window can be covered by 15 counters.

$7 \times 2 = 14$

The door can be covered by 14 counters.

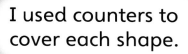

I used counters to cover each shape.

The window is larger because it has a larger area.

b) Another way to find the answer is to use different objects to measure area.

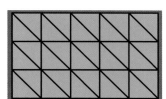

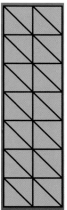

The window is covered by 30 triangles.
The door is covered by 28 triangles.

Think together

1 How many counters can you fit inside these shapes?

☐ counters fit inside the rectangle.

☐ counters fit inside the quadrilateral.

The shape with the larger space inside

is the _____ .

The shape with the larger area is

the _____ .

2 What is the area of this shape?

☐ triangles fit inside the rectangle.

The area of the rectangle is ☐ triangles.

3 Here are two rectangles.

A

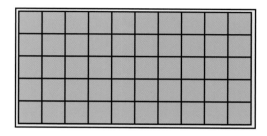

B

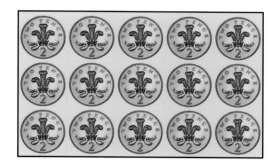

50 plastic squares

15 coins

Rectangle A is larger because 50 is more than 15.

I am not sure that is right.

Why does Astrid need to think again?

75

Counting squares ❶

Discover

❶ **a)** What is the area of each shape?

b) Draw a shape with an area in between the two sizes.

Share

a) The **units** we can use to measure area are squares.

Count the squares to find which shape is larger.

I drew lines to divide the shapes into squares. Then I wrote numbers inside to help me count them.

1	2	3
4	5	6
7	8	9

1
2

I wonder if it would help to place a counter on each square and then count them.

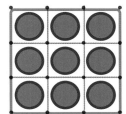

Shape A has an area of 9 squares (units).

Shape B has an area of 2 squares (units).

b) A shape with an area of between 2 and 9 squares will have an area of 3, 4, 5, 6, 7 or 8 squares.

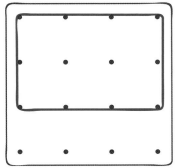

Think together

1 Count the squares in each shape to find the area.

Shape A   Shape B   Shape C

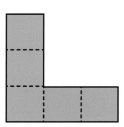   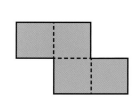   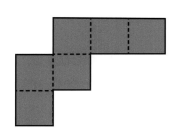

The area of Shape A is ☐ squares.

The area of Shape B is ☐ squares.

The area of Shape C is ☐ squares.

2 What is the area of these shapes?

A 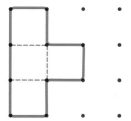   B 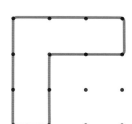   C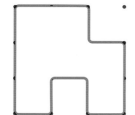

Shape	Area
A	
B	
C	

3 Ash has covered these rectangles with small paper squares.

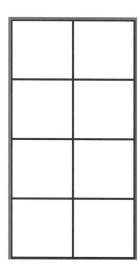

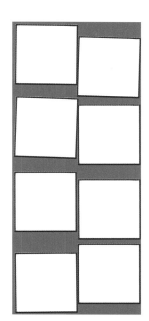

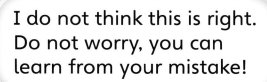

These rectangles both have an area of 8 squares.
They are the same size.

I do not think this is right. Do not worry, you can learn from your mistake!

What has Ash done wrong?

Explain why you think that this will give the wrong answer.

→ **Practice book 4B p57**

Counting squares ②

Discover

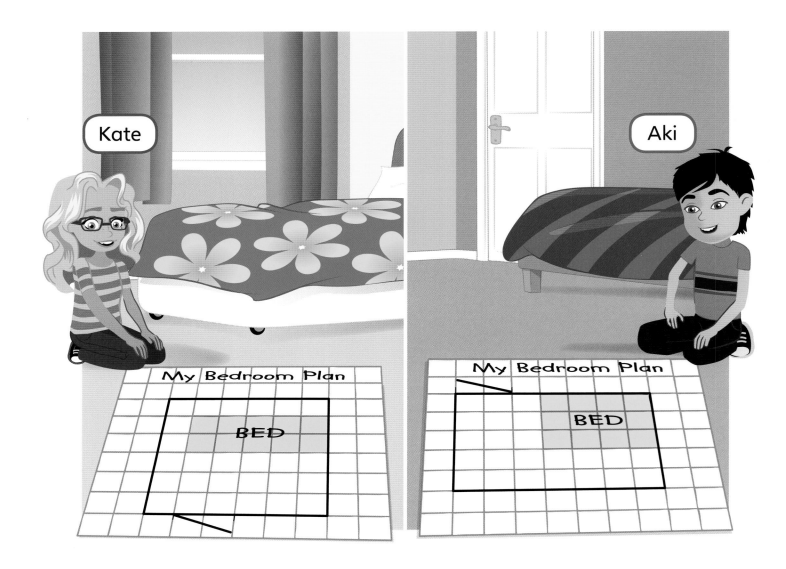

1 **a)** Who has the larger bed?

b) How much empty space do they both have in their bedroom?

Share

a) We can use squared paper to help find the area of different shapes.

> I numbered each square to make sure I did not miss any.

> I have thought of a way to use times-table facts to help.

1	2	3	4	5
6	7	8	9	10

1	2	3	4	5

Kate's bed has 2 rows of 5 squares. $2 × 5 = 10$

1	2	3	4
5	6	7	8
9	10	11	12

1	2	3	4

Aki's bed has 3 rows of 4 squares. $3 × 4 = 12$

12 squares is a larger area than 10 squares, so Aki's bed is larger.

b) Count the squares to find the area of the empty space.

1	2	3	4	5	6
7					
8					
9	10	11	12	13	14
15	16	17	18	19	20
21	22	23	24	25	26

1	2	3			
4	5	6			
7	8	9		
10	11	12	13	14	15	16
17	18	19	20	21	21	23

Kate has 26 squares of empty space in her bedroom.

Aki has 23 squares of empty space in his bedroom.

Think together

1 Find the areas of these three rectangles by counting the squares.

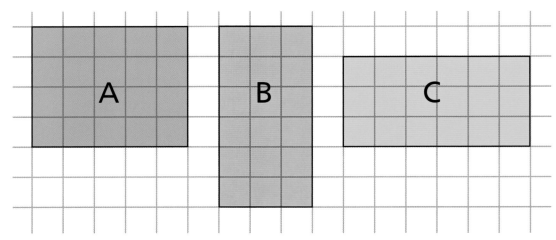

A = ⬚ squares   B = ⬚ squares   C = ⬚ squares

2 Work out the areas of these two rectilinear shapes.

A

B

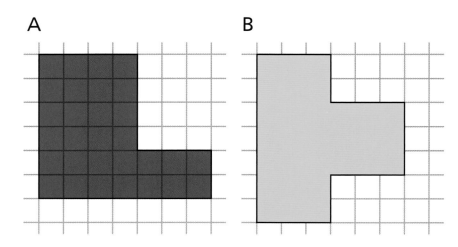

A rectilinear shape is a shape with straight sides that always meet at right angles. Squares and rectangles are rectilinear shapes.

A = ⬚ squares   B = ⬚ squares

3 Explain to a partner how you would calculate the area of the shaded shape.

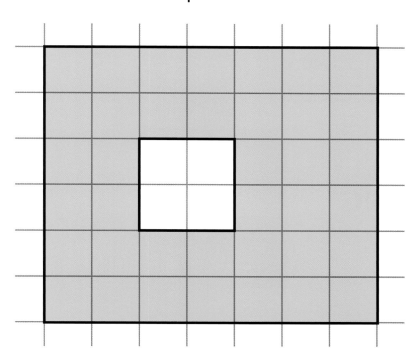

I found the area of this shape by counting squares.

I needed to use subtraction!

The area of this shape is ☐ squares.

→ Practice book 4B p60

Making shapes

Discover

1 **a)** What rectilinear shape of patio can you make with an area of 4 square slabs?

b) How can you make sure you have found every possible shape?

Share

a) When squares are used to make a rectilinear shape, they should touch at the side, not just the corner.

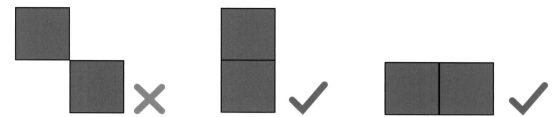

To show the patios with an area of 4 paving slabs, we can use 4 squares. They can be arranged in the following different ways.

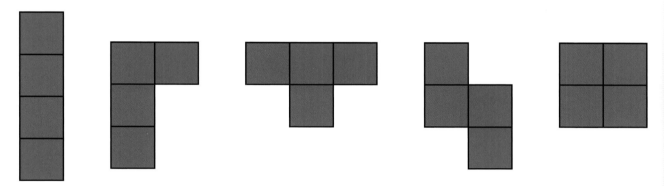

I made this shape too.

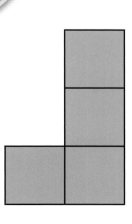

I will check to see if it really is a different shape.

85

b) Here is one way to find every possible shape.

Make a chain

(shape 1)

Move only 1 of the squares to begin with.

(shapes 2 and 3)

Then move 2 of the squares at a time.

(shapes 4 and 5)

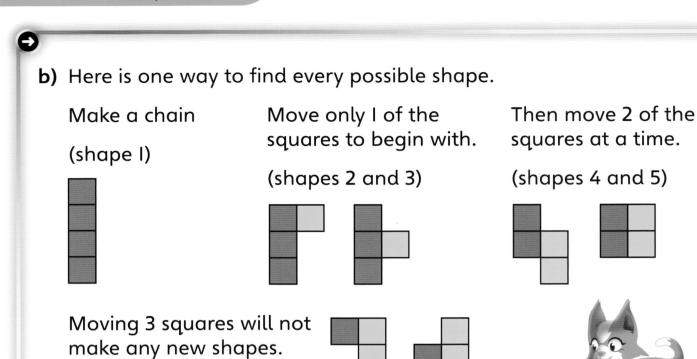

Moving 3 squares will not make any new shapes.

You might see other ways of moving squares but if they make reflections or rotations you do not count them!

Think together

1. Holly buys 2 packs of 4 square concrete slabs. She uses all of the slabs to make a patio.

   It is a rectilinear shape with an area of 8 square slabs.

   Place small paper squares on the grid to show two different patio shapes Holly could make. Draw your shapes on squared paper.

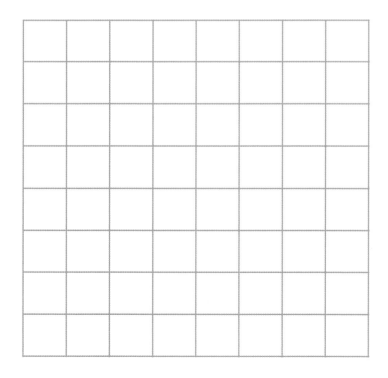

2 Look at the shapes you made for question 1. Move as few squares as you can to make two new patio shapes out of the 8 squares.

Draw your new shapes on squared paper.

3 Which one of these answers is the only shape that Holly can make for her rectilinear patio? Explain why.

CHALLENGE

A   B   C   D

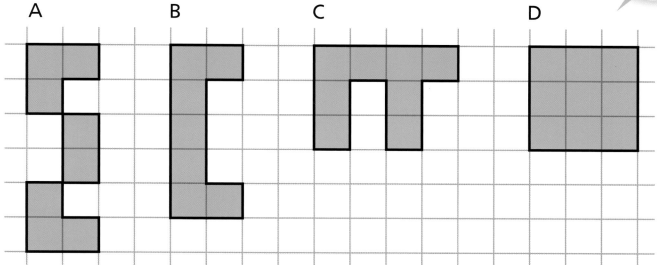

Hmmm … I think there is only one possible patio here.

You may be right, but how do you know? You need to explain your answer.

Comparing area

Discover

Danny

Olivia

The shape with the largest area wins!

I **a)** Who is winning the game? How do you know?

b) Which is larger: the area of the board that is covered or the area of the board that is not?

Share

a) The more squares that fit inside a shape, the larger its area.

Count the squares inside each shape.

Danny's red shape has an area of 16 squares.

Olivia's yellow shape has an area of 17 squares.

17 > 16, so Olivia is winning the game.

b)

> I am going to count all of the white squares.

> I will multiply to find the total area of the board. Then I will subtract the coloured squares.

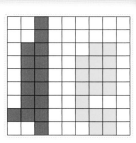

total area of the board

= 9 × 9

= 81

area of coloured squares

= 16 + 17

= 33

area of the white squares

= 81 − 33

= 48

The area of the board that is covered is 33 squares. The area that is not covered is 48 squares.

33 < 48

The area of the board that is not covered is larger.

Think together

1 Which shape has the larger area?

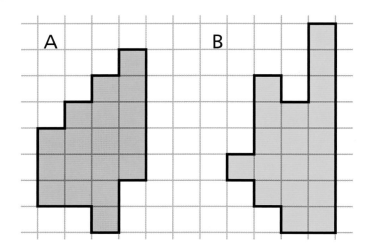

Area of A = ☐ squares.

Area of B = ☐ squares.

☐ > ☐

Shape ☐ has the larger area.

2 a) Find the area of each of these letters.

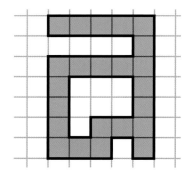
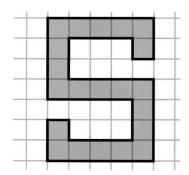
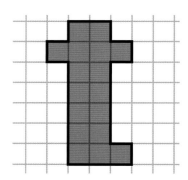

Letter a = ☐ squares

Letter s = ☐ squares

Letter t = ☐ squares

b) Put the letters in order of size, from smallest to largest area.

☐ , ☐ , ☐

3 The shape with the greater area wins. Who has won the game and why?

CHALLENGE

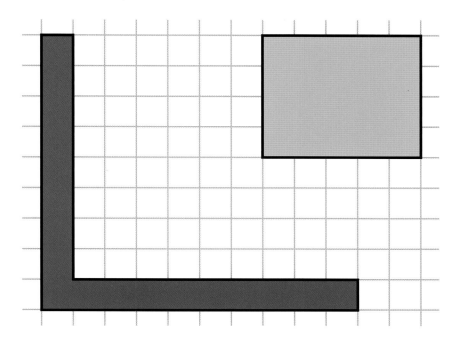

I win! My purple shape is a lot taller and wider than your rectangle, so the area must be greater.

I think we need to do something else to be able to compare areas.

Astrid

Flo

→ Practice book 4B p66

End of unit check

1 What is the area of a shape?

   A Area is the distance all the way around a shape.

   B Area is the length of a shape.

   C Area is the space inside a shape.

   D Area is the width of a shape.

2 What is the area of the rectangle?

   A 18 squares

   B 7 squares

   C 12 squares

   D 14 squares

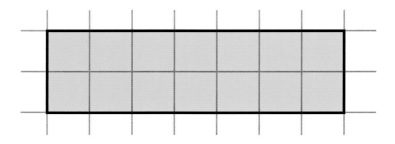

3 One of the shapes below does not have an area of 36 squares.
Which is it?

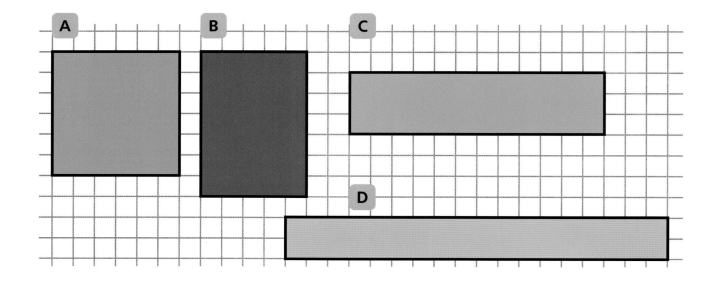

4 Which shape has the largest area?

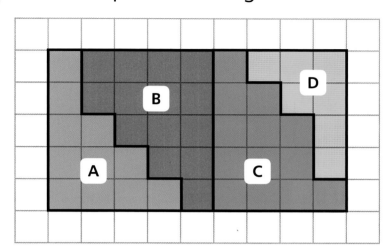

5 Which of these shapes is it not possible to make using 9 squares?

I square =

A   B   C   D

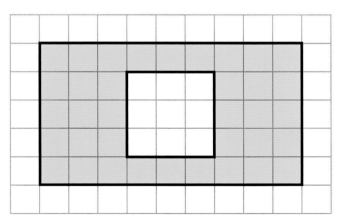

6 What is the area of the shaded shape?

The area of the shaded shape is ⬜ squares.

93

→ **Practice book 4B p69**

Unit 8
Fractions ❶

In this unit we will …

⚡ Find the links between tenths and hundredths

⚡ Identify equivalent fractions

⚡ Simplify fractions

⚡ Look at fractions that are greater than 1

How many tenths are shown here?

We will need some maths words.
Which of these have you met before?

tenths   **hundredths**   **equivalent**

simplify   **numerator**   **denominator**

fraction   **mixed number**

improper fraction   **simplest fraction**

Which one of these fractions is not equivalent to the others?

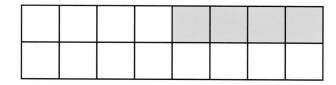

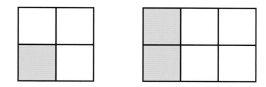

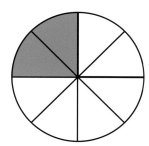

Tenths and hundredths ❶

Discover

❶ **a)** What fraction of the board is each square?

What fraction of the board has Danny covered with his counters?

b) What fraction of the board has Lexi covered with her counters?

Share

a) There are 100 squares. Each square is worth 1 **hundredth** ($\frac{1}{100}$).

Danny has covered 17 squares out of 100 or one full row and 7 extra squares.

As a fraction, this looks like: $\frac{17}{100}$.

Danny has covered $\frac{17}{100}$ of the board.

> There are 10 rows, so 1 row is $\frac{1}{10}$ of the board.

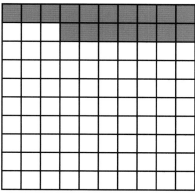

b) Lexi has covered 10 out of 100 squares.

This can be written as a fraction: $\frac{10}{100}$.

$\frac{10}{100} = \frac{1}{10}$

Lexi has covered $\frac{10}{100}$ or $\frac{1}{10}$ of the board.

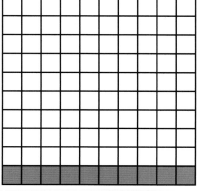

Think together

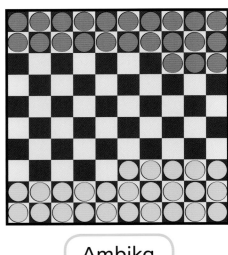

Max

1 Max and Ambika play next. The board looks like this.

a) What fraction of the board has Max covered?

There are 100 squares on the board.

Max has covered ☐ squares.

Max has covered $\frac{\square}{100}$ of the board.

Ambika

b) What fraction of the board has Ambika covered?

Ambika has covered ☐ squares.

Ambika has covered $\frac{\square}{\square}$ of the board.

c) What fraction of the board have Max and Ambika covered together?

Together they have covered $\frac{\square}{\square}$ of the board.

2 What fraction of each grid is shaded?

a)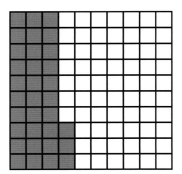

b)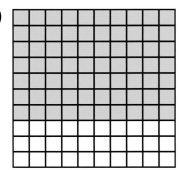

c)

98

3 Amelia and Richard played the board game.

Amelia scored $\frac{34}{100}$ and Richard scored $\frac{6}{10}$.

a) Show this with counters on a grid.

b) How many tenths and how many hundredths did Amelia score?

Amelia scored $\frac{\square}{10}$ and $\frac{\square}{100}$.

Richard

> I will start by counting how many full rows Amelia filled.

> I can show Amelia's score on a part-whole model.

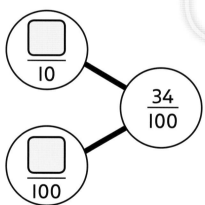

c) How many hundredths did Richard score?

Richard scored $\frac{\square}{100}$.

→ Practice book 4B p71

Tenths and hundredths ❷

Discover

We need to share this cake equally between 100 people.

1 **a)** Explain how the cake can be cut into 100 equal pieces.

What fraction of the cake is each piece?

b) 13 people eat a piece of cake.

What fraction of the cake has been eaten?

What fraction of the cake is now left?

Share

a) Cutting into 10 columns shows tenths.

Cutting each column into 10 rows shows hundredths.

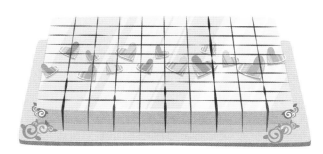

Each piece of cake is worth 1 hundredth ($\frac{1}{100}$).

b) 13 people ate a piece of cake. This means we need to count 13 hundredths.

I will use a fraction number line to help me.

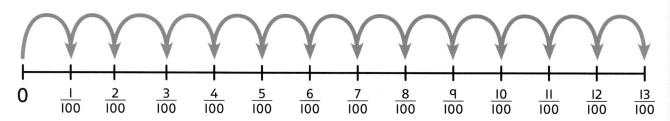

$\frac{13}{100}$ of the cake has been eaten.

$100 - 13 = 87$

There are 87 pieces of cake left.

There are $\frac{87}{100}$ of the cake left.

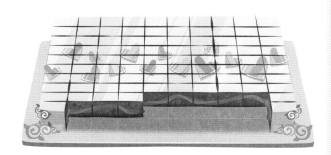

Think together

 The number line shows what fraction of the cake was eaten by 11 pm.

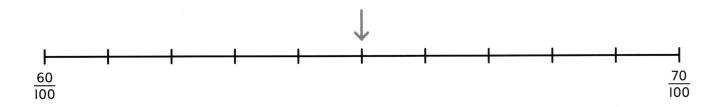

$$\frac{60}{100} \qquad\qquad\qquad\qquad\qquad\qquad\qquad\qquad \frac{70}{100}$$

a) What fraction of the cake was eaten by 11 pm?

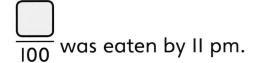

$\frac{\boxed{}}{100}$ was eaten by 11 pm.

b) Another 4 pieces were eaten by midnight.

What fraction of the cake was eaten by midnight?

$\frac{\boxed{}}{\boxed{}}$ was eaten by midnight.

Point to this fraction on the number line.

c) What fraction of the cake is left at midnight?

$100 - \boxed{} = \boxed{}$

There are $\frac{\boxed{}}{\boxed{}}$ of the cake left at midnight.

2 Work out the missing numbers on each fraction number line.

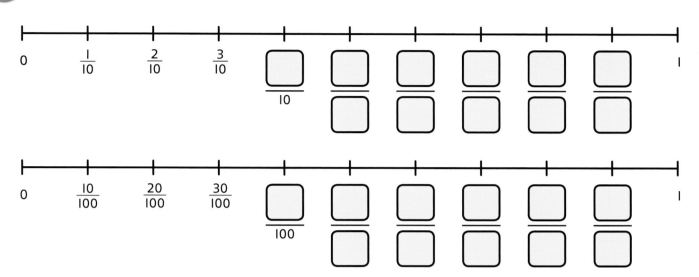

3 Emma and Jamie each have £1 (or 100 pence).

Emma and Jamie spend the following amounts of money.

CHALLENGE

Emma

Jamie

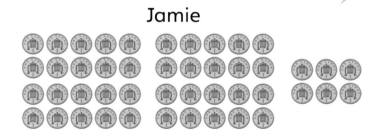

a) Mark on the fraction number line the fraction of £1 that each person has spent.

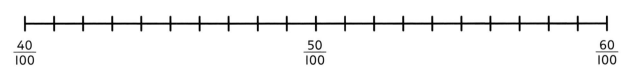

$\frac{40}{100}$ $\qquad$ $\frac{50}{100}$ $\qquad$ $\frac{60}{100}$

b) What is the same about the fraction of money each person has spent?

c) What fraction of money does each person have left?

→ **Practice book 4B p74**

Equivalent fractions ①

Discover

Olivia

Max

① **a)** Use the fraction wall to show that $\frac{1}{3}$ is equivalent to $\frac{2}{6}$.

What other fraction on the wall is equivalent to $\frac{1}{3}$?

b) Max says that $\frac{3}{4}$ is equivalent to $\frac{4}{6}$.

Use the fraction wall to decide whether Max is correct.

Share

a) Look at the fraction wall to see which fractions line up with each other.

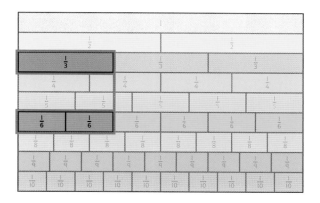 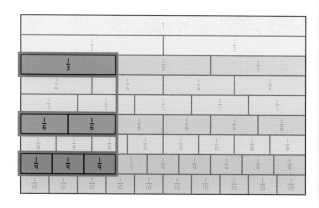

$\frac{1}{3}$ is equivalent to $\frac{2}{6}$.

$\frac{1}{3}$, $\frac{2}{6}$ and $\frac{3}{9}$ are equivalent.

> 3, 6 and 9 are all in the 3 times-table!

b) The fraction wall can help us see if these fraction are the same or not.

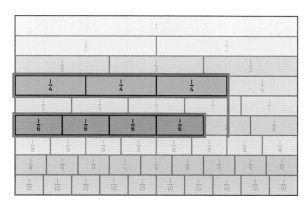

> I can use the signs < and > to write a number sentence about these fractions: $\frac{3}{4} > \frac{4}{6}$ or $\frac{4}{6} < \frac{3}{4}$.

$\frac{3}{4}$ and $\frac{4}{6}$ do not line up on the fraction wall.

$\frac{3}{4}$ is not equivalent to $\frac{4}{6}$.

Max is incorrect.

Think together

1. Which of the following statements are true and which are false? Circle the correct answers. Explain how you know.

a)

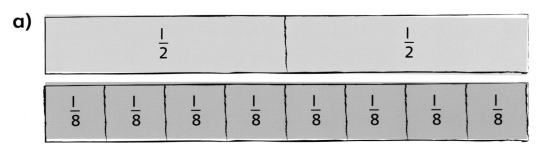

$\frac{1}{2}$ is equal to $\frac{2}{8}$. This is true / false

because _____ .

b)

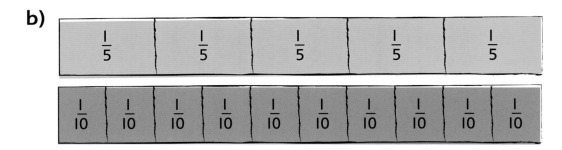

$\frac{2}{10}$ is the same as $\frac{1}{5}$. This is true / false

because _____ .

c)

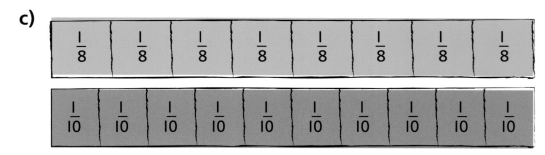

$\frac{4}{8}$ and $\frac{4}{10}$ are equivalent fractions. This is true / false

because _____ .

2 Write down the fractions equivalent to $\frac{1}{2}$. How many can you find?

$\frac{1}{2}$			$\frac{1}{2}$		
$\frac{1}{3}$	$\frac{1}{3}$	$\frac{1}{3}$
$\frac{1}{4}$	$\frac{1}{4}$	$\frac{1}{4}$	$\frac{1}{4}$
$\frac{1}{5}$	$\frac{1}{5}$	$\frac{1}{5}$	$\frac{1}{5}$	$\frac{1}{5}$
$\frac{1}{6}$	$\frac{1}{6}$	$\frac{1}{6}$	$\frac{1}{6}$	$\frac{1}{6}$	$\frac{1}{6}$
$\frac{1}{8}$	$\frac{1}{8}$	$\frac{1}{8}$	$\frac{1}{8}$	$\frac{1}{8}$	$\frac{1}{8}$	$\frac{1}{8}$	$\frac{1}{8}$
$\frac{1}{10}$	$\frac{1}{10}$	$\frac{1}{10}$	$\frac{1}{10}$	$\frac{1}{10}$	$\frac{1}{10}$	$\frac{1}{10}$	$\frac{1}{10}$	$\frac{1}{10}$	$\frac{1}{10}$

3 Match the pairs of equivalent fractions. You can use the fraction wall from question 2 to help you.

CHALLENGE

A 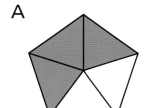 B 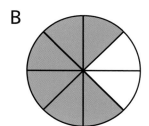 C 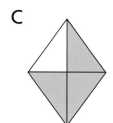 D

I will start by working out what fraction of each shape is shaded.

→ **Practice book 4B p77**

Equivalent fractions ❷

Discover

"Sort them into two groups of equivalent fractions."

1 **a)** Sort the cards into two groups of equivalent fractions.

b) Here are three cards from another set of equivalent fractions.

What are the missing numbers?

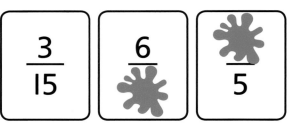

Share

a)

I can see if the fractions are the same by dividing up a rectangle.

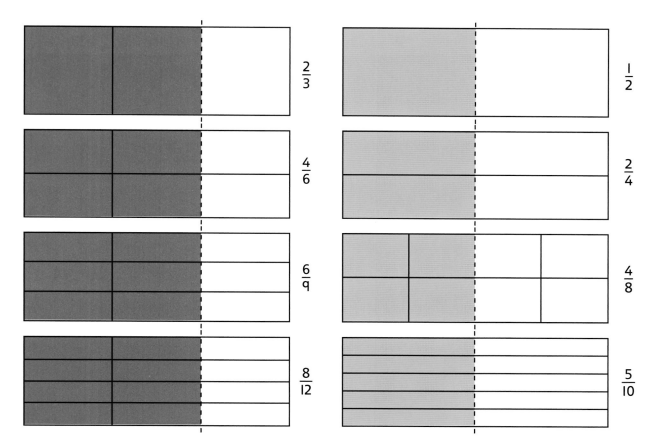

$\frac{2}{3}$

$\frac{4}{6}$

$\frac{6}{9}$

$\frac{8}{12}$

$\frac{1}{2}$

$\frac{2}{4}$

$\frac{4}{8}$

$\frac{5}{10}$

I will compare the numerators and the denominators to see what similarities they have.

b) We need to multiply the numerator and denominator by 2.

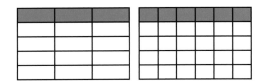

$$\frac{3}{15} = \frac{6}{30}$$

× 2 / × 2

I used my knowledge of times-tables: 3 × 2 = 6, so I multiplied 15 by 2.

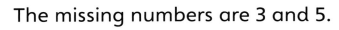

We need to divide the numerator and denominator by 3.

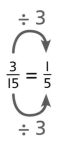

÷ 3

$$\frac{3}{15} = \frac{1}{5}$$

÷ 3

15 ÷ 5 = 3, so I think that this time we need to divide the numerator and denominator.

The missing numbers are 3 and 5.

Think together

1 Match the pairs of equivalent fractions.

$\frac{1}{3}$

$\frac{6}{15}$

$\frac{2}{7}$

$\frac{2}{5}$

$\frac{10}{35}$

$\frac{3}{9}$

2 Isla has paired up some fraction cards.

Some of the numbers are covered.

$$\frac{1}{4}$$ = $$\frac{3}{\text{🌸}}$$ $$\frac{3}{5}$$ = $$\frac{\text{🌸}}{20}$$ $$\frac{\text{🌸}}{8}$$ = $$\frac{12}{16}$$

What are the missing numbers?

3 Andy has these two fraction cards. $$\frac{6}{10}$$ $$\frac{9}{15}$$

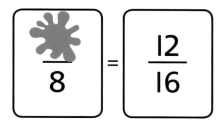

These two fractions are not equal. You do not multiply the numerator and denominator by the same number.

Andy

I think they are equal.

a) Explain how Jamie is correct.

Jamie

b) Write down three more fractions that are equivalent to the two fractions shown.

I will draw some diagrams to help me.

I will divide the numerator and denominators first. This might show me whether they are the same.

III

→ **Practice book 4B p80**

Simplifying fractions

Discover

Mo

Lexi

1 **a)** What fraction of Mo's picture is shaded?

Is there more than one answer?

b) What fraction of Lexi's picture is shaded?

What is the **simplest fraction** you can find?

Share

a) In Mo's picture, 6 out of 9 squares are shaded ($\frac{6}{9}$).

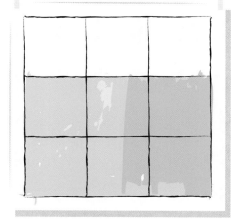

You can also see that $\frac{2}{3}$ of the shape is shaded. There are 3 rows in total and 2 rows are shaded.

$$\overset{\div 3}{\frown}$$
$$\frac{6}{9} = \frac{2}{3}$$
$$\underset{\div 3}{\smile}$$

$\frac{2}{3}$ of Mo's picture is shaded.

b) $\frac{16}{20}$ of Lexi's picture is shaded.

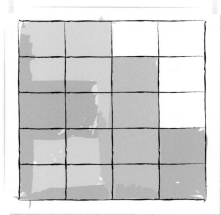

I need to find a number that divides into both the numerator and denominator. I can divide by 2 and then 2 again.

I think that it is quicker to divide by 4.

$$\overset{\div 2 \quad \div 2}{\frown \quad \frown} \qquad \overset{\div 4}{\frown}$$
$$\frac{16}{20} = \frac{8}{10} = \frac{4}{5} \qquad \frac{16}{20} = \frac{4}{5}$$
$$\underset{\div 2 \quad \div 2}{\smile \quad \smile} \qquad \underset{\div 4}{\smile}$$

$\frac{4}{5}$ is the simplest fraction.

In the simplest fraction, there are no numbers that divide into both the numerator and the denominator.

Think together

1   Look at Isla's picture.

What fraction of Isla's picture is shaded?

$\dfrac{\boxed{}}{12}$ of Isla's picture is shaded.

Write the fraction in its simplest form.

$\dfrac{\boxed{}}{\boxed{}}$

When you **simplify** a fraction, you are making the fraction numbers as small as possible. For example, $\frac{4}{8} = \frac{2}{4} = \frac{1}{2}$

2   In a car park there are 15 cars.

5 of the cars are yellow and 6 of the cars are red.

a) What fraction of the cars are yellow? Find the simplest fraction.

$\div 5$

$\dfrac{5}{15} = \dfrac{\boxed{}}{\boxed{}}$

$\div 5$

$\dfrac{\boxed{}}{\boxed{}}$ of the cars are yellow.

b) What fraction of the cars are red? Find the simplest fraction.

$\dfrac{\boxed{}}{\boxed{}} = \dfrac{\boxed{}}{\boxed{}}$

$\dfrac{\boxed{}}{\boxed{}}$ of the cars are red.

3 Andy and Reena have both shaded part of a rectangle.

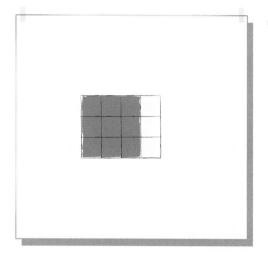

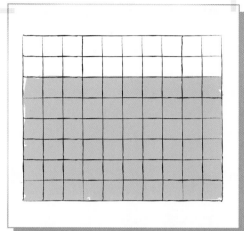

I think we have shaded the same fraction of our shape.

That is not possible. I have shaded more squares.

Andy

Reena

Who is correct? Explain your reasoning.

I will write each fraction and then simplify them.

→ **Practice book 4B p83**

Fractions greater than 1 **❶**

Discover

❶ a) How many whole hexagons can Jamilla and Richard make?

How many triangles will be left over?

b) Write the total number of hexagons as a fraction.

Share

a)

I counted up in 6s until there were no more triangles left.

Jamilla and Richard can make 4 whole hexagons.

They will have 5 triangles left over.

b)

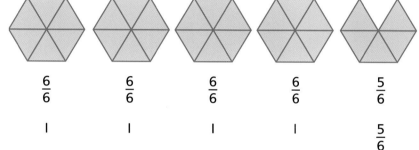

$\frac{6}{6}$ $\frac{6}{6}$ $\frac{6}{6}$ $\frac{6}{6}$ $\frac{5}{6}$

1   1   1   1 $\frac{5}{6}$

There are 4 whole hexagons and one with $\frac{5}{6}$.

There are $4\frac{5}{6}$ hexagons.

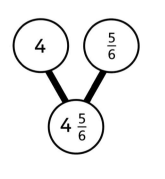

I can write the number of whole hexagons and the fraction of a hexagon in a part-whole model.

A number with wholes and a fraction is called a mixed number.

Think together

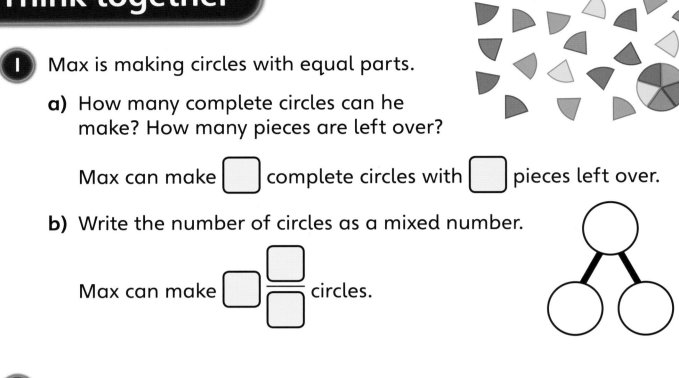

1 Max is making circles with equal parts.

a) How many complete circles can he make? How many pieces are left over?

Max can make ☐ complete circles with ☐ pieces left over.

b) Write the number of circles as a mixed number.

Max can make ☐ $\frac{☐}{☐}$ circles.

2 Lexi and Amelia made rectangles from small squares.

How many rectangles did each person make?

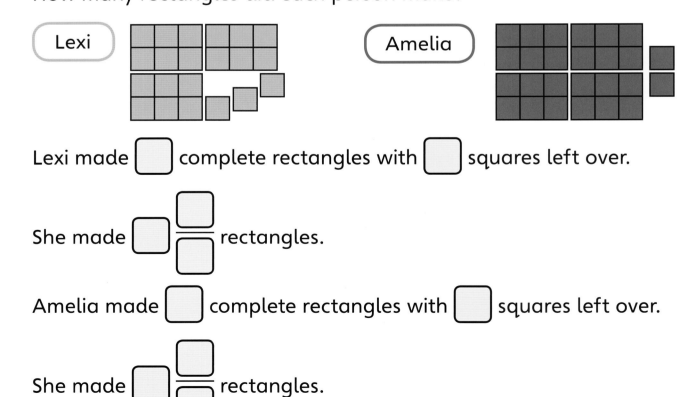

Lexi

Amelia

Lexi made ☐ complete rectangles with ☐ squares left over.

She made ☐ $\frac{☐}{☐}$ rectangles.

Amelia made ☐ complete rectangles with ☐ squares left over.

She made ☐ $\frac{☐}{☐}$ rectangles.

3 Olivia is tidying away some toy cubes.

8 cubes fit into one box.

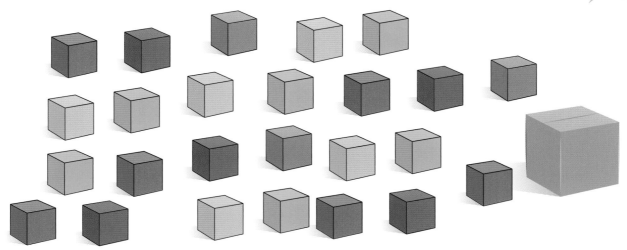

a) How many boxes can Olivia fill completely? ⬜ boxes

b) How many cubes will be left over?

⬜ will be left over.

c) Write the boxes of cubes as a mixed number.

There will be ⬜ ⬜/⬜ boxes of cubes.

I wonder what multiplication facts will help.

119

→ **Practice book 4B p86**

Fractions greater than 1 ❷

Discover

1 **a)** 7 runners each take a bottle of water.

How many whole packs are needed?

What fraction of the next pack is needed?

b) How many packs are needed in total?

Write your answer in two ways.

Share

a) There are 5 bottles of water in each pack. Count in fifths.

Make 7 jumps, 1 for each runner.

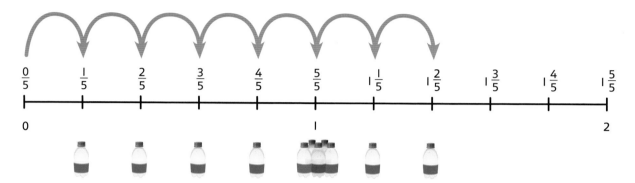

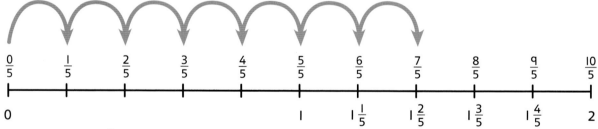

1 whole pack and $\frac{2}{5}$ of the next pack are needed.

b) Answer 1: $1\frac{2}{5}$ packs are needed in total.

Use a number line to see another way of writing this number.

This shows $\frac{7}{5}$.

$1\frac{2}{5} = \frac{7}{5}$

Answer 2: $\frac{7}{5}$ packs are needed in total.

$1\frac{2}{5}$ is a mixed number. It has a whole (1) and a part $\frac{2}{5}$.

$\frac{7}{5}$ is an improper fraction. The numerator is larger than the denominator.

Think together

1 9 people took an energy bar at the next station.

How many packs of energy bars were eaten?

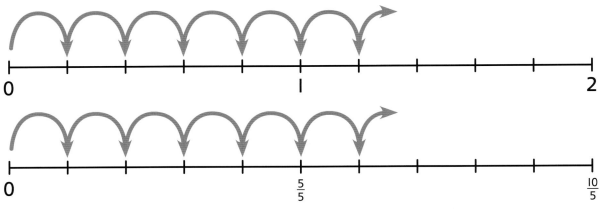

Write your answer in two ways.

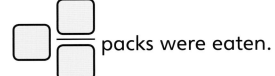 packs were eaten.

$\boxed{}$ of a pack was eaten.

2 Kate walks $\frac{1}{4}$ of a kilometre (km) every day.

How far does Kate walk in 11 days?

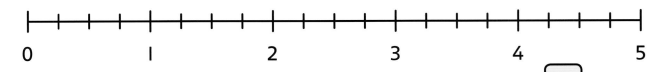

Write your answer as a mixed number. Kate walks $\boxed{}\boxed{\frac{}{}}$ km.

Write your answer as an improper fraction. Kate walks $\boxed{\frac{}{}}$ km.

3 Here are three number lines.

a) Point to where $1\frac{6}{9}$ appears on each number line.

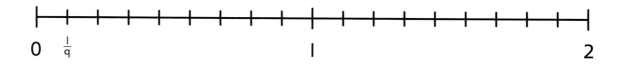

0    $\frac{1}{9}$ 1   2

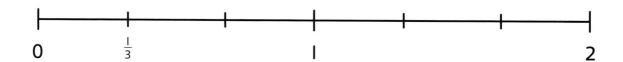

0              $\frac{1}{3}$ 1   2

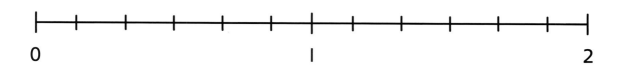

0   1   2

b) Write $1\frac{6}{9}$ in as many other ways as you can.

I can write it as an improper fraction.

I will use my knowledge of equivalent fractions to find other ways.

123

End of unit check

1 What fraction is shaded?

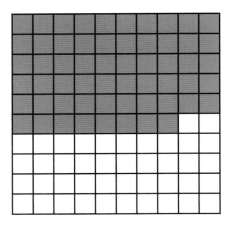

A 58

B $\frac{58}{10}$

C $\frac{58}{100}$

D $\frac{5}{10}$

2 Which fraction is not equivalent to $\frac{1}{2}$?

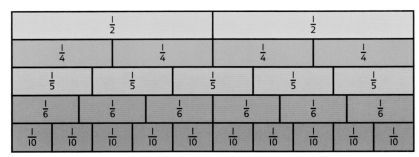

A $\frac{2}{4}$

B $\frac{2}{5}$

C $\frac{3}{6}$

D $\frac{5}{10}$

3 What fraction is shaded?

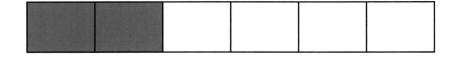

A $\frac{2}{4}$

B $\frac{1}{3}$

C $\frac{2}{3}$

D $\frac{1}{q}$

4 What is $\frac{20}{24}$ in its simplest form?

A $\frac{5}{6}$ **B** $\frac{10}{12}$ **C** $\frac{1}{6}$ **D** $\frac{1}{5}$

5 Which fraction is the same as this?

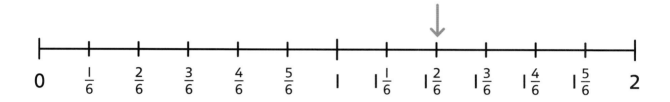

| 0 | $\frac{1}{6}$ | $\frac{2}{6}$ | $\frac{3}{6}$ | $\frac{4}{6}$ | $\frac{5}{6}$ | 1 | $1\frac{1}{6}$ | $1\frac{2}{6}$ | $1\frac{3}{6}$ | $1\frac{4}{6}$ | $1\frac{5}{6}$ | 2 |

A $\frac{2}{6}$ **B** $\frac{1}{3}$ **C** $\frac{8}{6}$ **D** $\frac{12}{6}$

6 These two shapes need the same fraction shaded.

How many squares should be shaded in the rectangle?

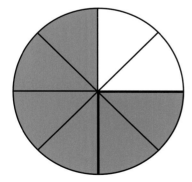
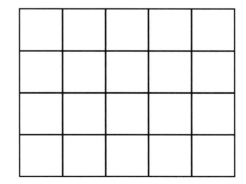

Explain your reasoning.

→ **Practice book 4B p92**

Unit 9
Fractions ②

In this unit we will …

⚡ Learn to add and subtract fractions with the same denominator

⚡ Learn to subtract a fraction from a whole number

⚡ Understand how to find a fraction of an amount

We will use fraction strips to add and subtract fractions.

$\frac{3}{8} + \frac{1}{8} = \frac{4}{8}$

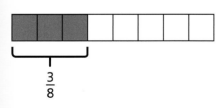

$\frac{3}{8}$

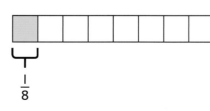

$\frac{1}{8}$

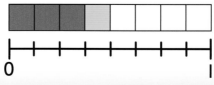

0   1

We will need some maths words. How many of these do you remember?

numerator   **denominator**   **add**

subtract   **improper fraction**

mixed number   **fraction of an amount**

You need to be able to find a fraction of an amount.

Find $\frac{2}{3}$ of 24

$24 \div 3 = 8$

$8 \times 2 = 16$

$\frac{2}{3}$ of 24 is 16

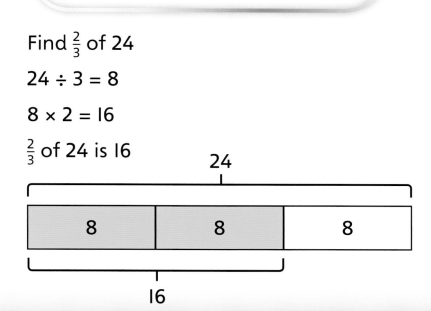

24

| 8 | 8 | 8 |

16

Adding fractions

Discover

I have eaten $\frac{4}{5}$ of my pizza.

I have eaten $\frac{3}{5}$ of my pizza.

Kate

Luis

1 **a)** What fraction of pizza have Kate and Luis eaten in total?

b) Kate's friends drink $\frac{7}{10}$ of a litre of juice.

Luis's friends drink $\frac{9}{10}$ of a litre of juice.

How much juice do they drink in total?

Share

a) Kate has eaten $\frac{4}{5}$ of her pizza.

Luis has eaten $\frac{3}{5}$ of his pizza.

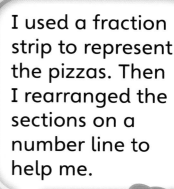

I used a fraction strip to represent the pizzas. Then I rearranged the sections on a number line to help me.

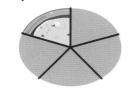

$\frac{4}{5}$

$\frac{3}{5}$

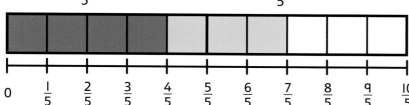

$$\frac{4}{5} + \frac{3}{5} = \frac{7}{5}$$

| 0 | $\frac{1}{5}$ | $\frac{2}{5}$ | $\frac{3}{5}$ | $\frac{4}{5}$ | $\frac{5}{5}$ | $\frac{6}{5}$ | $\frac{7}{5}$ | $\frac{8}{5}$ | $\frac{9}{5}$ | $\frac{10}{5}$ |

Kate and Luis have eaten $\frac{7}{5}$ in total.

b)

$\frac{7}{10}$

$\frac{9}{10}$

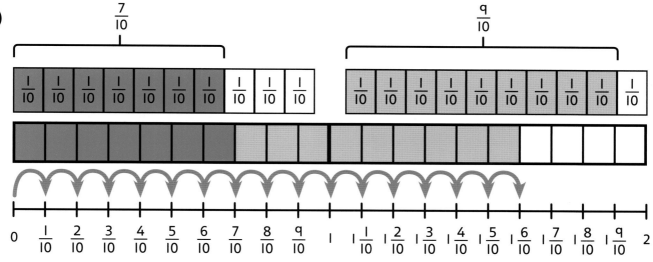

| 0 | $\frac{1}{10}$ | $\frac{2}{10}$ | $\frac{3}{10}$ | $\frac{4}{10}$ | $\frac{5}{10}$ | $\frac{6}{10}$ | $\frac{7}{10}$ | $\frac{8}{10}$ | $\frac{9}{10}$ | 1 | $1\frac{1}{10}$ | $1\frac{2}{10}$ | $1\frac{3}{10}$ | $1\frac{4}{10}$ | $1\frac{5}{10}$ | $1\frac{6}{10}$ | $1\frac{7}{10}$ | $1\frac{8}{10}$ | $1\frac{9}{10}$ | 2 |

$\frac{7}{10}$ of a litre $+ \frac{9}{10}$ of a litre $= 1\frac{6}{10}$ litres

Kate's and Luis's friends drink $1\frac{6}{10}$ litres in total.

You can write your answer as a mixed number ($1\frac{6}{10}$) or an improper fraction ($\frac{16}{10}$).

129

Think together

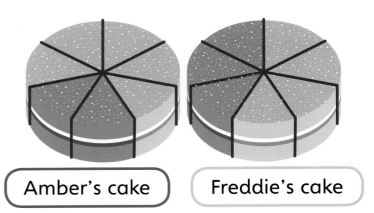

1 $\frac{5}{7}$ of Amber's cake is eaten.

$\frac{4}{7}$ of Freddie's cake is eaten.

What fraction of cake has been eaten altogether?

Amber's cake   Freddie's cake

$\frac{5}{7} + \frac{4}{7} = \dfrac{\boxed{}}{\boxed{}}$

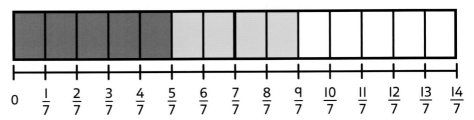

$\dfrac{\boxed{}}{\boxed{}}$ of cake is eaten altogether.

2 Max walks $\frac{8}{9}$ km. He then walks a further $\frac{7}{9}$ km.

How far does Max walk in total?

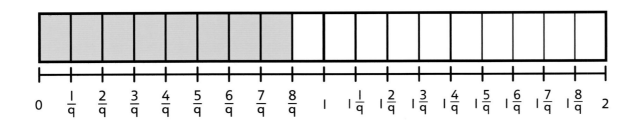

$\frac{8}{9} + \dfrac{\boxed{}}{\boxed{}} = \dfrac{\boxed{}}{\boxed{}}$

I add the numerators because the denominators are equal.

Max walks $\dfrac{\boxed{}}{\boxed{}}$ or $1\dfrac{\boxed{}}{\boxed{}}$ km in total.

3 Here are some fraction cards.

| $\frac{3}{8}$ | $\frac{1}{8}$ | $\frac{7}{8}$ | $\frac{5}{8}$ | $\frac{9}{8}$ |

a) Name two cards that have a sum of $\frac{10}{8}$.

b) Which three cards will have the greatest total?

c) Name two cards that make a whole when added together.

d) What is the sum of all five cards?

I think there may be more than one correct answer to some of these questions.

I used a number line to help me. I can see more than one way to write my answer. A whole is the same as $\frac{8}{8}$.

131

→ **Practice book 4B p94**

Subtracting fractions ❶

Discover

❶ **a)** Olivia uses $\frac{3}{4}$ kg of spaghetti to make a meal.

How much spaghetti is left?

b) Does Olivia have enough spaghetti to make the same meal again tomorrow?

Share

a)

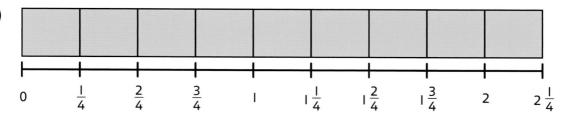

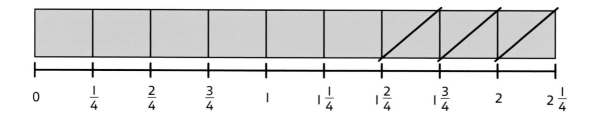

I used a fraction strip to represent the spaghetti and then crossed out $\frac{3}{4}$ to see what was left.

$2\frac{1}{4}$ kg $- \frac{3}{4}$ kg $= 1\frac{2}{4}$ kg

There are $1\frac{2}{4}$ kg of spaghetti left.

b)

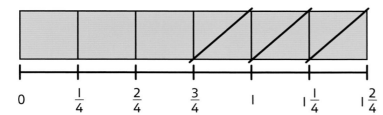

$1\frac{2}{4}$ kg $- \frac{3}{4}$ kg $= \frac{3}{4}$ kg

Olivia has enough spaghetti to make the same meal again tomorrow.

Think together

1 Jude has $3\frac{1}{5}$ litres of water. He drinks $\frac{4}{5}$ of a litre of water.

How much water is left?

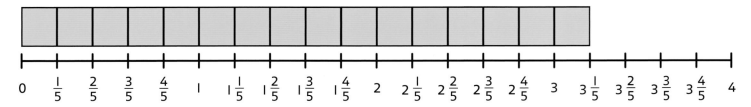

$$3\frac{1}{5} - \frac{4}{5} = \boxed{}\,\frac{\boxed{}}{\boxed{}}$$

There are $\boxed{}\,\frac{\boxed{}}{\boxed{}}$ litres of water left.

2 The distance from Mawusi's school to her home is $2\frac{3}{8}$ km.

So far she has walked $\frac{5}{8}$ km.

How much further does she need to walk?

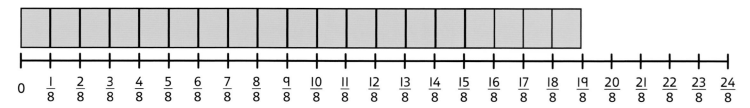

$$2\frac{3}{8} - \frac{\boxed{}}{\boxed{}} = \boxed{}\,\frac{\boxed{}}{\boxed{}}$$

Mawusi has to walk $\boxed{}\,\frac{\boxed{}}{\boxed{}}$ km further.

3 **a)** Work out the answers to these calculations.

$1\frac{2}{7} - \frac{5}{7}$ $\qquad$ $\frac{9}{7} - \frac{5}{7}$

What is the same and what is different about these two questions?

b) Work out the answers to these calculations.

$1\frac{1}{9} - \frac{5}{9}$

$1\frac{1}{9} - \frac{6}{9}$

$1\frac{1}{9} - \frac{7}{9}$

$1\frac{1}{9} - \frac{8}{9}$

Explain the pattern in the answers.

c) How many ways can you find to complete the missing numbers?

$3\frac{\boxed{}}{6} - \frac{\boxed{}}{6} = 2\frac{1}{6}$

I will make fraction strips to help me find different answers.

135

→ **Practice book 4B p97**

Subtracting fractions ❷

Discover

Sophia

Cheese and tomato pizza

Mushroom pizza

① **a)** Sofia sells 2 slices of cheese and tomato pizza.

What fraction of cheese and tomato pizza does she have left?

b) Sofia sells some slices of mushroom pizza.

She has 2 $\frac{1}{6}$ mushroom pizzas left.

How many slices did she sell?

Share

a) There are 2 cheese and tomato pizzas, each cut into 6 pieces.

2 slices have been sold.

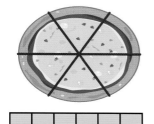 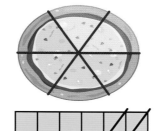

> I left 1 pizza as a whole and took 2 slices away from the second pizza.

$2 - \frac{2}{6} = 1\frac{4}{6}$

or

$2 - \frac{2}{6} = 1\frac{6}{6} - \frac{2}{6} = 1\frac{4}{6}$

Sofia has $1\frac{4}{6}$ cheese and tomato pizzas left.

b) There were 3 mushroom pizzas to start with.

Now there are only $2\frac{1}{6}$ left.

> I know 3 pizzas each cut into 6 slices is $\frac{18}{6}$.

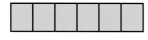  

$3 - \frac{5}{6} = 2\frac{1}{6}$

There is $\frac{5}{6}$ less mushroom pizza than we started with.

Sofia sold 5 slices of pizza.

Think together

1 Holly cooks 3 pizzas for her family. She eats $\frac{2}{3}$ of a pizza.

How many pizzas does she have left?

$$3 - \frac{2}{3} = 2\frac{\square}{\square} - \frac{\square}{\square}$$

$$= \square\frac{\square}{\square}$$

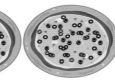

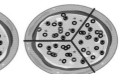

Holly has $\square\frac{\square}{\square}$ pizzas left for her family.

2 Abdul orders 8 pizzas for a party.

He eats $\frac{3}{5}$ of a pizza before his friends arrive.

How many pizzas are left for his friends?

$$8 - \frac{\square}{\square} = \square\frac{\square}{\square} - \frac{\square}{\square}$$

$$= \square\frac{\square}{\square}$$

There are $\square\frac{\square}{\square}$ pizzas left for Abdul's friends.

3 There are 5 cheese and tomato pizzas and 5 mushroom pizzas for a party.

Each pizza is cut into 7 slices.

a) Some of the cheese and tomato pizza is eaten.

There are $4\frac{2}{7}$ cheese and tomato pizzas remaining.

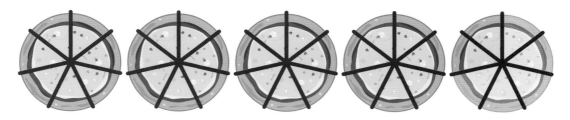

What fraction of cheese and tomato pizza has been eaten?

$\frac{\Box}{\Box}$ of a cheese and tomato pizza has been eaten.

b) Some mushroom pizza is eaten by 2 people.

There are now $4\frac{2}{7}$ mushroom pizzas left.

How much mushroom pizza has been eaten?

How many ways could it have been shared between 2 people?

I will use fraction strips to represent the pizzas.

139

→ **Practice book 4B p100**

Problem solving – adding and subtracting fractions ❶

Discover

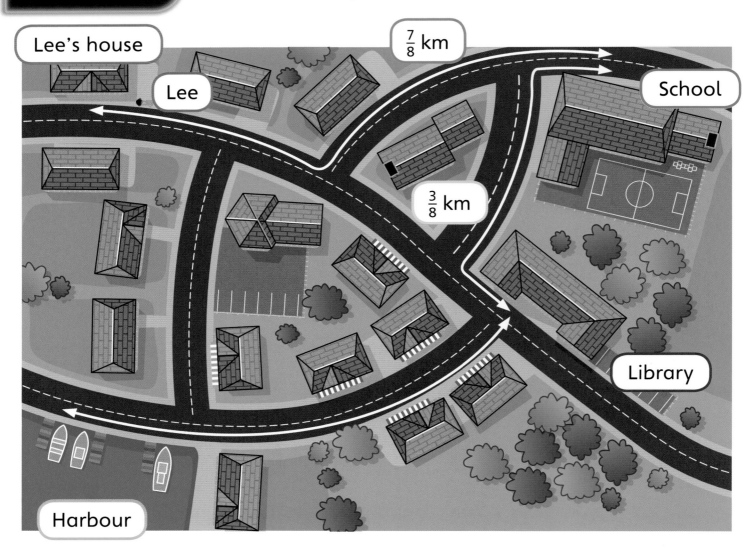

❶ **a)** Lee walks from his house to school and then to the library.

How far does he walk in total?

b) Lee then walks to the harbour. In total, he has now walked 2 km.

How far is it from the library to the harbour?

140

Share

a) The map shows the distances between each building.

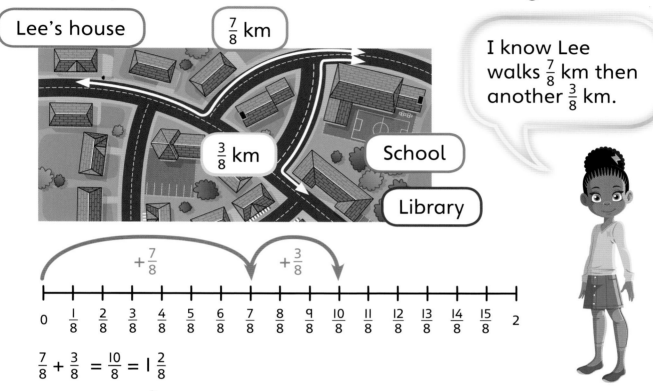

Lee's house

$\frac{7}{8}$ km

$\frac{3}{8}$ km

School

Library

I know Lee walks $\frac{7}{8}$ km then another $\frac{3}{8}$ km.

$+\frac{7}{8}$ $+\frac{3}{8}$

0 $\frac{1}{8}$ $\frac{2}{8}$ $\frac{3}{8}$ $\frac{4}{8}$ $\frac{5}{8}$ $\frac{6}{8}$ $\frac{7}{8}$ $\frac{8}{8}$ $\frac{9}{8}$ $\frac{10}{8}$ $\frac{11}{8}$ $\frac{12}{8}$ $\frac{13}{8}$ $\frac{14}{8}$ $\frac{15}{8}$ 2

$\frac{7}{8} + \frac{3}{8} = \frac{10}{8} = 1\frac{2}{8}$

Lee walks $1\frac{2}{8}$ km in total.

b) Lee has now walked 2 km in total.

$$2 = 1\frac{8}{8}$$

$$1\frac{8}{8} - 1\frac{2}{8} = \frac{6}{8}$$

I will do a subtraction to work out how much more Lee has to travel. He has already walked $1\frac{2}{8}$ km.

It is $\frac{6}{8}$ km from the library to the harbour.

$\frac{6}{8}$ km

Library

Harbour

Think together

1 Ogenna, Robert and Aisha are all friends.

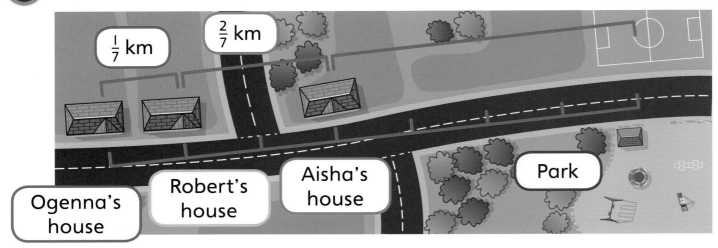

$\frac{1}{7}$ km $\frac{2}{7}$ km

Ogenna's house   Robert's house   Aisha's house   Park

Ogenna walks from her house to Robert's house, then to Aisha's house and then to the park. In total she walks 1 km. How far is the park from Aisha's house?

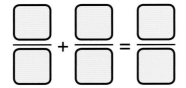

$$\frac{\square}{\square} + \frac{\square}{\square} = \frac{\square}{\square}$$

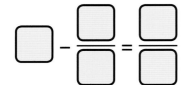

$$\square - \frac{\square}{\square} = \frac{\square}{\square}$$

The park is $\frac{\square}{\square}$ km away from Aisha's house.

2 Here are five pieces of ribbon.

Aaron wants 1 m of ribbon. Find how he can make this total using:

a) 1 piece of ribbon

b) 2 pieces of ribbon

c) 3 pieces of ribbon.

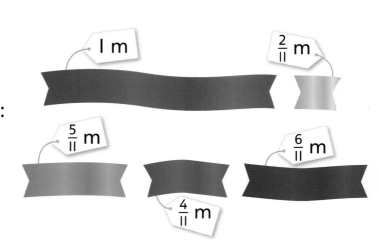

1 m $\frac{2}{11}$ m $\frac{5}{11}$ m $\frac{6}{11}$ m $\frac{4}{11}$ m

142

3 Max, Lexi, Amelia, Jamie and Danny have run 3 km between them, to raise money for charity.

I have run $\frac{4}{5}$ km.

Max

I have run the same distance as Danny.

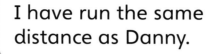

Jamie

I have run $\frac{3}{5}$ km.

Amelia

I have run $\frac{2}{5}$ km more than Max.

Lexi

I have run the same distance as Jamie.

Danny

How far did Jamie and Danny run?

I will start by working out the total distance that Max, Lexi and Amelia have run.

I wonder if a number line would help.

143

→ **Practice book 4B p103**

Problem solving – adding and subtracting fractions ❷

Discover

I used $\frac{3}{7}$ of a metre of ribbon to wrap the larger present.

Aki

I used $\frac{2}{7}$ of a metre of ribbon to wrap the smaller present.

Bella

1 **a)** Aki and Bella had 2 m of ribbon before they started wrapping presents.

How much ribbon do they have left after wrapping the two presents?

b) They wrap one more present using $\frac{4}{7}$ m of ribbon.

How much ribbon is left now?

Share

a) $\frac{3}{7} + \frac{2}{7} = \frac{5}{7}$

> I will add the two lengths together to see how much ribbon they have used so far. Then I will subtract from 2.

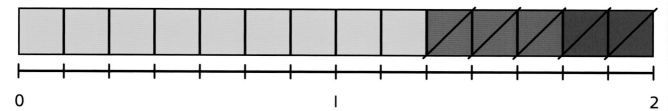

0　　　　　　　　1　　　　　　　　2

Aki and Bella use $\frac{5}{7}$ m of the ribbon in total.

The ribbon is 2 m long before they start wrapping presents.

$2 - \frac{5}{7} = 1\frac{7}{7} - \frac{5}{7} = 1\frac{2}{7}$

There are $1\frac{2}{7}$ m of the ribbon left.

b) Aki and Bella wrap another present using $\frac{4}{7}$ m of ribbon.

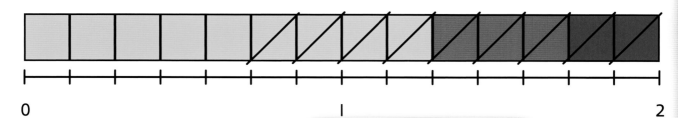

0　　　　　　　　1　　　　　　　　2

$\frac{5}{7} + \frac{4}{7} = \frac{9}{7} = 1\frac{2}{7}$

$2 - 1\frac{2}{7} = \frac{5}{7}$

> I subtracted the whole I first and then $\frac{2}{7}$ from the remaining whole.

There is $\frac{5}{7}$ m of ribbon left.

145

Think together

1 Here are three jugs of juice.

$\frac{4}{10}$ full $\frac{3}{10}$ full $\frac{2}{10}$ full

Richard wants to pour all the juice into I jug. Will it fit?

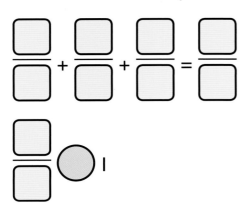

$\frac{\square}{\square} + \frac{\square}{\square} + \frac{\square}{\square} = \frac{\square}{\square}$

$\frac{\square}{\square} \bigcirc 1$

> I think I need to put a sign in the circle. Is the amount of juice greater (>) or less (<) than I?

The juice _____ all fit into I jug.

2 Here are three more jugs of juice.

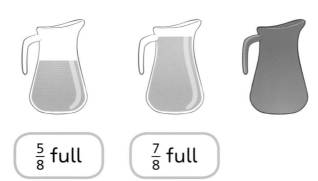

$\frac{5}{8}$ full $\frac{7}{8}$ full

The jugs are all poured together and completely fill 2 jugs.

What fraction of the third jug is filled with juice?

The third jug is $\frac{\square}{\square}$ filled with juice.

3 Max is trying to work out the answer to this problem.

$$\frac{1}{5} + \frac{3}{4} + \frac{4}{5} + \frac{1}{4}$$

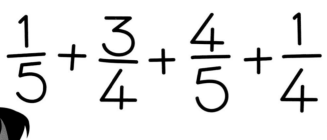

Max

I do not think I can do this. I can only add fractions with the same denominator.

How could Max add the fractions together?

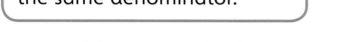

It must be possible. I just do not know how to do it!

I remember that I can add numbers in any order. Maybe if I rearrange the order of the fractions this will help.

147

→ **Practice book 4B p106**

Calculating fractions of a quantity

Discover

The largest doll is 24 centimetres tall.

1 **a)** The smallest doll is $\frac{1}{8}$ of the height of the largest doll.

How tall is the smallest doll?

b) The middle doll is $\frac{3}{8}$ of the height of the largest doll.

How tall is the middle doll?

Share

a) The largest doll is 24 cm tall.

I will split my fraction strip into 8 sections because I need to work out $\frac{1}{8}$.

24 cm

| $\frac{1}{8}$ | $\frac{1}{8}$ | $\frac{1}{8}$ | $\frac{1}{8}$ | $\frac{1}{8}$ | $\frac{1}{8}$ | $\frac{1}{8}$ | $\frac{1}{8}$ |

? cm

24 cm

| 3 | 3 | 3 | 3 | 3 | 3 | 3 | 3 |

3 cm

$24 ÷ 8 = 3$, so the smallest doll is 3 cm tall.

b)

24 cm

| 3 | 3 | 3 | 3 | 3 | 3 | 3 | 3 |

9 cm

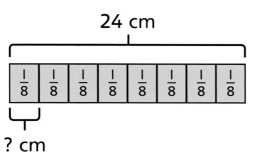

$24 ÷ 8 = 3$, so $\frac{1}{8} = 3$ cm

$3 × 3$ cm $= 9$ cm, so $\frac{3}{8} = 9$ cm

The middle doll is 9 cm tall.

If I know $\frac{1}{8}$ is 3 cm, I can multiply this by 3 to find $\frac{3}{8}$.

Think together

1 A toy train is 60 cm long. The engine is $\frac{1}{5}$ of the train's length.

How long is the engine?

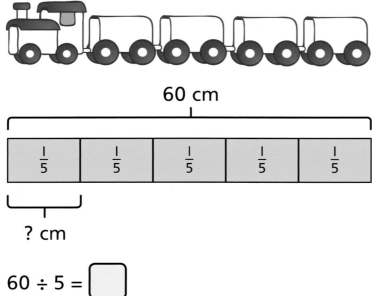

60 ÷ 5 = ☐

The engine is ☐ cm long.

2 Danisha has a 30 cm ruler, a pencil and a rubber.

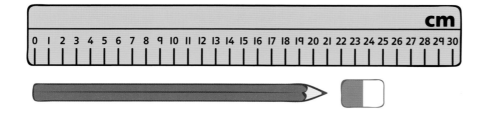

a) The rubber is $\frac{1}{10}$ of the length of the ruler.

How long is the rubber?

b) The pencil is $\frac{7}{10}$ of the length of the ruler.

How long is the pencil?

3 Work out the answers to these questions.

$\frac{1}{3}$ of 15 cm = ☐ cm

$\frac{1}{5}$ of 15 cm = ☐ cm

$\frac{3}{7}$ of £42 = £ ☐

> I am going to draw fraction strips to show that my answers are correct.

4 Who has more money, Aki or Ebo?

CHALLENGE

> I have $\frac{3}{4}$ of £24.

> I have $\frac{3}{8}$ of £24.

Aki

Ebo

> I do not need to draw a diagram. I know Ebo has more because 8 is bigger than 4!

Is Dexter correct?

151

Problem solving – fraction of a quantity ❶

Discover

There is $\frac{1}{3}$ of the jar left.

Reena

❶ **a)** There are 200 g of jam left in the jar.

How many grams of jam are in the jar when it is full?

b) Reena eats 60 g of cheese.

$\frac{3}{5}$ of the block of cheese is left.

How many grams of cheese are left?

Share

a) There are 200 g of jam left in the jar.

I think there are 3 lots of this amount in a full jar.

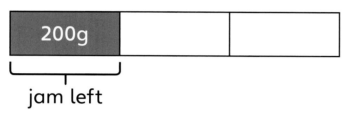

jam left

200 g × 3 = 600 g

There are 600 g of jam in the jar when it is full.

b) $\frac{3}{5}$ of the block of cheese is left.

This means that Reena has eaten $\frac{2}{5}$ of the block.

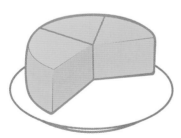

I know that 2 parts represent 60 g of cheese.

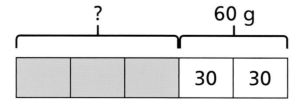

60 ÷ 2 = 30

30 × 3 = 90

There are 90 g of cheese left.

153

Think together

1   Rebecca has a bottle of juice.

There is $\frac{1}{5}$ left in the bottle.

There are 100 ml left.

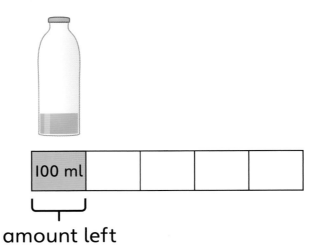

amount left

How much juice was in the bottle when it was full?

☐ × 100 = ☐ ml

A full bottle has ☐ ml of juice.

2   Erik eats $\frac{2}{7}$ of a packet of sweets.

There are 35 sweets left in the packet.

How many sweets were in it when it was full?

35 ÷ ☐ = ☐

☐ × ☐ = ☐

A full packet of sweets has ☐ sweets.

> I know $1 - \frac{2}{7} = \frac{5}{7}$ and I will use this information to help me work out the answer.

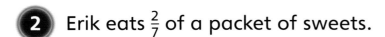

154

3 Lexi and Andy each have a box of chocolates.

Who had more chocolates in their box to start with?

I have eaten $\frac{3}{7}$ of my chocolates.

I have eaten $\frac{5}{8}$ of my chocolates.

Lexi

Andy

28 chocolates left   15 chocolates left

28

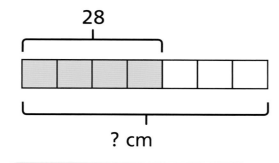

? cm

? cm

Lexi's chocolates box

Andy's chocolates box

How many sevenths do Lexi's 28 chocolates represent?

I am going to work out what fraction of the box Andy has left.

155

→ Practice book 4B p112

Problem solving – fraction of a quantity ❷

Discover

I have 30 cubes.

Danny

We have the same number of red cubes.

Lee

1 **a)** $\frac{2}{5}$ of Danny's tower is made of red cubes.

How many red cubes are in Danny's tower?

b) $\frac{3}{4}$ of Lee's tower is made of red cubes.

Whose tower has more cubes?

How many more cubes does it have?

Share

a) Danny has 30 cubes in his tower.

$\frac{2}{5}$ of the cubes are red.

$30 \div 5 = 6$

$2 \times 6 = 12$

There are 12 red cubes in Danny's tower.

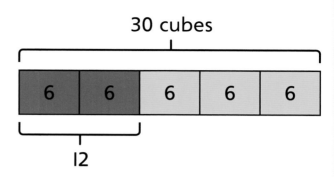

30 cubes

| 6 | 6 | 6 | 6 | 6 |

12

b) Lee has the same number of red cubes as Danny, which is 12.

The 12 red cubes are $\frac{3}{4}$ of Lee's tower.

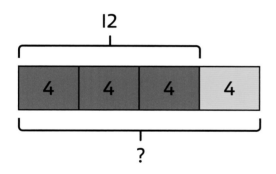

12

| 4 | 4 | 4 | 4 |

?

I need to work out how many cubes there are in Lee's tower in total. I can do this by finding $\frac{1}{4}$ first, then multiplying this by 4.

$12 \div 3 = 4$

Each part of the fraction strip is worth 4 cubes.

$4 \times 4 = 16$

There are 16 cubes in Lee's tower.

Danny's tower has 30 cubes, so Danny's tower has more cubes.

$30 - 16 = 14$

Danny's tower has 14 more cubes than Lee's tower.

Think together

I Danny and Lee have each made another tower of cubes.

They each use 24 cubes in their tower.

> $\frac{1}{6}$ of my tower is made of red cubes.

> $\frac{5}{8}$ of my tower is made of red cubes.

Danny

Lee

How many more red cubes does Lee have than Danny?

$24 \div 6 = \boxed{}$

Danny's tower has $\boxed{}$ red cubes.

$24 \div 8 = \boxed{}$

$\boxed{} \times 5 = \boxed{}$

Lee's tower has $\boxed{}$ red cubes.

$\boxed{} - \boxed{} = \boxed{}$

Lee's tower has $\boxed{}$ more red cubes than Danny's tower.

> I will work out the unit fractions of red cubes for both towers.

> I will draw a fraction strip to help me work out how many red cubes Lee's tower has.

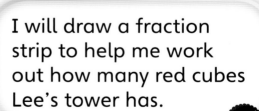

2 Danny's tower and Lee's tower both have 18 red cubes.

$\frac{3}{8}$ of my tower is made of red cubes.

$\frac{9}{10}$ of my tower is made of red cubes.

Danny

Lee

Which tower has more cubes?

How many more cubes does the taller tower have?

_____'s tower has more cubes. It has ⬜ more cubes.

3 There are 80 flowers.

$\frac{1}{4}$ of the flowers are red roses.

$\frac{3}{10}$ of the remaining flowers are yellow roses.

The rest of the flowers are white roses.

How many of each type of flower are there?

CHALLENGE

I wonder if you can use one fraction strip to find the solution.

I worked out how many red roses there are and then how many are not red.

159

→ **Practice book 4B p115**

End of unit check

1 Find the answer to the following calculation.

$$\frac{5}{8} + \frac{7}{8}$$

A 12 **B** $\frac{12}{16}$ **C** $\frac{12}{8}$ **D** $1\frac{2}{8}$

2 Find the answer to the following calculation.

$$3 - \frac{2}{5}$$

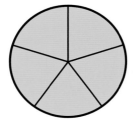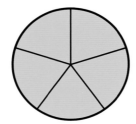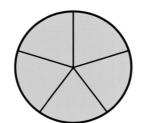

A $3\frac{2}{5}$ **B** $2\frac{3}{5}$ **C** 1 **D** $\frac{1}{5}$

3 Mark bakes some bread.

He has $2\frac{1}{3}$ kg flour.

A loaf of bread needs $\frac{2}{3}$ kg of flour.

How much flour does he have left?

A $1\frac{1}{3}$ kg **B** 3 kg **C** $1\frac{2}{3}$ kg **D** 2 kg

4 Harry has 45 apples.

He uses $\frac{3}{5}$ of them to make some juice.

How many apples does he have left?

A $\frac{2}{5}$ **B** 27   **C** 18   **D** 75

5 Jane takes part in a cycle race.

She cycles 64 km.

This is $\frac{2}{3}$ of the total distance.

How long is the cycle race?

A 96 km   **B** 64 km   **C** 42 km   **D** 21 km

6 Ambika spends $\frac{2}{5}$ of her money on a new T-shirt.

How much money does she have left?

Ambika has £ ☐ left.

£20

161

→ Practice book 4B p118

Unit 10
Decimals ❶

In this unit we will ...

⚡ Learn about the decimal point, and tenth and hundredth columns

⚡ Explore tenths and hundredths as decimals

⚡ Understand how to divide 1- and 2-digit numbers by 10 and 100

⚡ Complete calculations resulting in a decimal answer

Here is a place value grid. What columns have we used before? What columns are new? Is there anything else we have not seen before?

T	O	•	Tth	Hth
1	2	•	3	4

We will need some maths words.
Which words have you seen before?

tens   ones   decimal point

tenths   hundredths   greater than

equivalent   less than

decimal   centimetre   millimetre

We will need this too!
What should be shown at X?

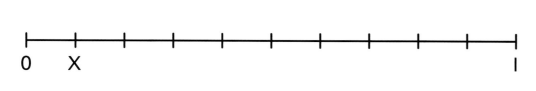

Tenths ❶

Discover

❶ a) Which ten frame could represent the fraction $\frac{5}{10}$?

b) Is there another way to represent $\frac{5}{10}$ as a number?

Share

a) The ten frame is the whole. Each ten frame is split into 10 equal parts.

In $\frac{5}{10}$, the denominator is 10 and the numerator is 5.

The ten frame that represents $\frac{5}{10}$ is the one with counters on 5 of the 10 parts.

$\frac{1}{10}$	$\frac{1}{10}$	$\frac{1}{10}$	$\frac{1}{10}$	$\frac{1}{10}$
$\frac{1}{10}$	$\frac{1}{10}$	$\frac{1}{10}$	$\frac{1}{10}$	$\frac{1}{10}$

b) $\frac{5}{10}$ is read as 5 tenths.

T	O	•	Tth
		•	$\frac{1}{10}$ $\frac{1}{10}$ $\frac{1}{10}$ $\frac{1}{10}$ $\frac{1}{10}$
	0	•	5

We can write $\frac{5}{10}$ as a **decimal**.

The **decimal point** separates the ones and tenths column.

This can be represented as 5 counters in the tenths column on a place value grid.

There are 0 ones and 5 tenths.

$\frac{5}{10}$ can be written as 0·5

Think together

1 Represent the following fractions on a ten frame and on a place value grid. Write the decimal equivalent.

a) $\frac{3}{10} = $ ⬜.⬜

b) $\frac{6}{10} = $ ⬜.⬜

= 1 whole

T	O	•	Tth
		•	
		•	

2 What fraction is shown by the shaded and unshaded counters?

How could these fractions be written as decimals?

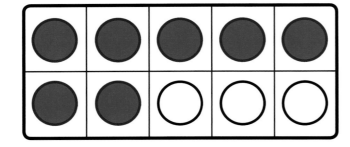

The shaded counters show $\frac{⬜}{⬜}$. This can be written as ⬜.⬜ .

The unshaded counters show $\frac{⬜}{⬜}$. This can be written as ⬜.⬜ .

CHALLENGE

3 **a)** Max is counting in tenths from 0·5.

Identify the mistake he has made.

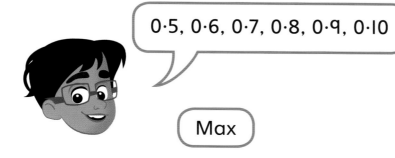

0·5, 0·6, 0·7, 0·8, 0·9, 0·10

Max

b) Amelia and Olivia are both counting in tenths at the same time and speed.

Amelia starts at 0 and counts upwards.

Olivia starts at 1 and counts downwards.

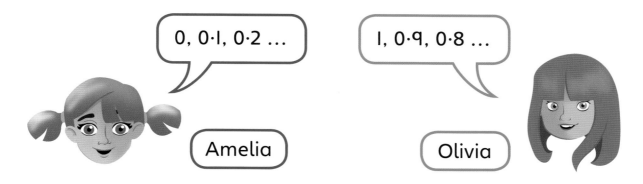

0, 0·1, 0·2 …

1, 0·9, 0·8 …

Amelia

Olivia

Will both children say the same number at the same time?

I will use a number line to help me to count in tenths. I wonder what comes after 1.

I am going to try to count up in steps of 0·2 now.

167

→ **Practice book 4B p120**

Tenths ②

Discover

0·3 m   2·3 m   3·1 m   1·3 m

1 **a)** Write and represent the height values on a place value grid.

b) Where would the heights be placed on this number line?

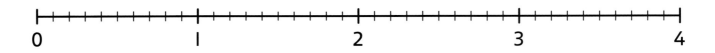

0   1   2   3   4

Share

a) 0·3 is 0 ones and 3 tenths.

2·3 is 2 ones and 3 tenths.

3·1 is 3 ones and 1 tenth.

1·3 is 1 one and 3 tenths.

O	•	Tth
0	•	$\frac{1}{10}$ $\frac{1}{10}$ $\frac{1}{10}$ 3
① ① 2	•	$\frac{1}{10}$ $\frac{1}{10}$ $\frac{1}{10}$ 3
① ① ① 3	•	$\frac{1}{10}$ 1
① 1	•	$\frac{1}{10}$ $\frac{1}{10}$ $\frac{1}{10}$ 3

b) The smallest number is 0·3 and the largest number is 3·1.

I will use the value of each digit from a) to help me position each number on the number line.

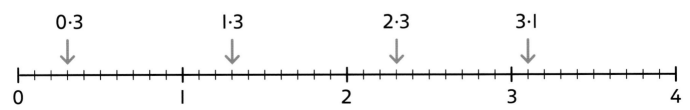

169

Think together

1 **a)** What number is represented here?

O	•	Tth
①	•	$\frac{1}{10}$ $\frac{1}{10}$ $\frac{1}{10}$

 ☐.☐ is shown.

b) Use counters to represent 3·4.

O	•	Tth
	•	

2 Danny and Zac are counting together in tenths.

Not all of the numbers that they say are the same. The final number they should say is shown on the ten frames.

Who is correct? What mistakes did the other person make?

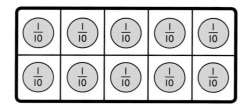

0, 0·1, 0·2, 0·3, 0·4, 0·5, 0·6, 0·7, 0·8, 0·9, 0·10, 0·11, 0·12

Danny

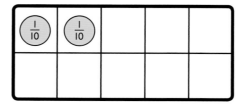

0, 0·1, 0·2, 0·3, 0·4, 0·5, 0·6, 0·7, 0·8, 0·9, 1·0, 1·1, 1·2

Zac

3 Find the answers. Do not use the same digit card twice in one question.

CHALLENGE

| 1 | 5 | 0 | 3 | 9 |

a) What is the largest number that can be made?

☐ ☐ . ☐

b) What is the smallest number that can be made?

☐ . ☐

c) What is the closest number to 50 that can be made?

☐ ☐ . ☐

d) Find two numbers that lie between 31 and 32.

☐ ☐ . ☐

☐ ☐ . ☐

Maybe I can do this in more than one way.

I wonder what the value of each digit is in the numbers I make.

171

Tenths ③

Discover

1 **a)** How long is the beetle?

How can this length be represented as a fraction and as a decimal?

b) A caterpillar measures 0·7 cm longer than the beetle.

How long is the caterpillar?

Share

> $\frac{1}{10}$ of a centimetre (cm) is called a millimetre (mm).

a) The beetle is between 3 cm and 4 cm long.

Each centimetre is split into 10 equal parts.

Each part is $\frac{1}{10}$ of a cm.

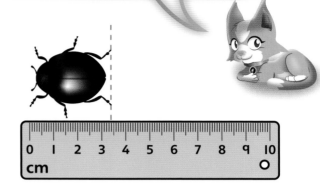

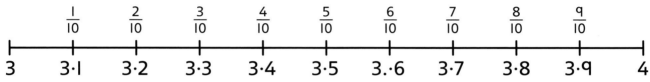

The end of the beetle is 4 parts further than 3 cm.

The beetle is $3\frac{4}{10}$ cm long. This can also be written as 3·4 cm.

b) 0·7 cm longer means making 7 jumps of 0·1 cm along the ruler.

We can count on in tenths.

> I am going to use a number line to find the length of the caterpillar!

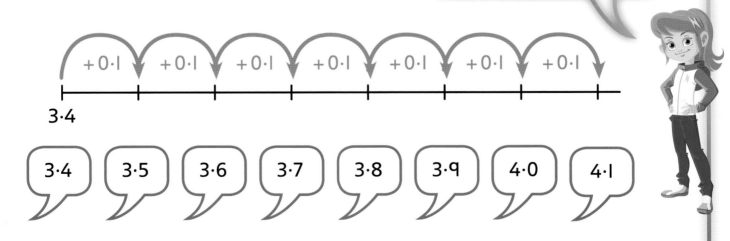

The caterpillar is 4·1 cm long.

Think together

1 Tom has walked $3\frac{1}{2}$ km of his 4 km journey to school.

a) Where on the number line would Tom be?

Tom's house   school

0   4 km

b) How could the distance Tom has travelled be written as a number with a decimal place?

Tom has travelled ☐.☐ km.

2 Two children have written different answers to show the length of the centipede below.

Explain why they are both correct.

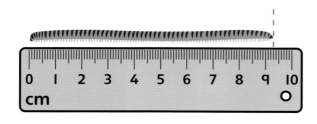

I think the centipede is $9\frac{3}{10}$ cm long.

Aki

I think the centipede is 9·3 cm long.

Ambika

3 Ambika and Emma are both counting at the same speed.

Ambika starts at 2 and counts on in tenths.

2, 2·1, 2·2, 2·3 ...

Ambika

Emma starts at 9 and counts backwards in tenths.

9, 8 $\frac{9}{10}$, 8 $\frac{8}{10}$ ...

Emma

a) What number will they say at the same time?

How might each child represent this number?

I wonder if there is a quicker way to calculate the answer without counting every step.

Using a ruler as a number line might help you to find the solution.

b) When Ambika says 3·8, what will Emma say?

175

→ **Practice book 4B p126**

Dividing by 10 ❶

Discover

I need to cut this piece of rope into 10 equally-sized pieces to tie off the sails.

Holly

❶ a) The piece of rope is 3 m long.

How long would each new piece of rope be?

b) What calculation can be written to show what Holly has done?

What does each number in the calculation represent?

Share

a) Each counter represents 1 m.

O	•	Tth
① ① ①	•	

We cannot divide 3 counters into 10 parts so we need to exchange each 1 for 10 tenths.

Each counter now represents $\frac{1}{10}$ or 0·1 of a metre.

We can divide the 30 counters into 10 parts.

30 tenths ÷ 10 = 3 tenths.

So, each new piece of rope would be $\frac{3}{10}$ of a metre, or 0·3 m long.

O	•	Tth
	•	(grid of tenths counters)

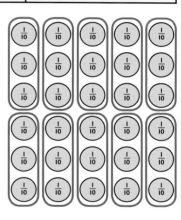

I have noticed that each piece of rope is $\frac{1}{10}$ of the size of the original piece of rope.

b) The calculation that shows what Holly has done is: 3 ÷ 10 = 0·3.

The 3 represents the length in metres of the original piece of rope.

The 10 represents the number of pieces this rope is cut into.

The 0·3 represents the length of each new piece of rope.

Think together

1 There are 4 kg of sweets in a bag.

The sweets are shared equally between 10 bowls.

What mass of sweets will there be in each bowl?

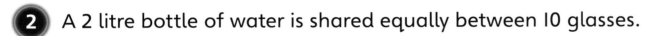

O	•	Tth
① ① ① ①	•	

O	•	Tth
	•	

☐ tenths ÷ 10 = ☐ tenths.

There will be ☐·☐ kg of sweets in each bowl.

2 A 2 litre bottle of water is shared equally between 10 glasses.

What volume of water will be in each glass?

☐ ÷ ☐ = ☐

There will be ☐·☐ litres of water in each glass.

> I will visualise a place value grid to help me to complete the calculation mentally.

3 A section of a fence is made out of 10 equally sized panels.

The section of fence is 9 m long.

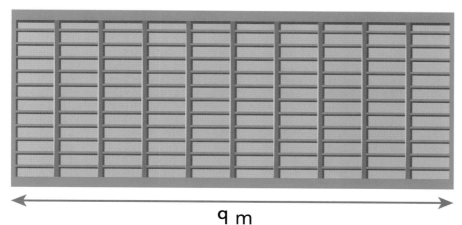

9 m

Tom has tried to find the length of each panel.

His calculation is shown below.

$10 \div 9 = 1.1$

a) Spot where the mistake has been made.

b) How could using counters help Tom to find the correct answer?

I will start with the whole length of the fence. I will use counters to show tenths, so I can group the counters into 10 panels.

I think each fence panel should be less than 1 m.

179

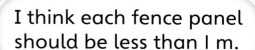→ **Practice book 4B p129**

Dividing by 10 ②

Discover

If there are 10 books with the same mass in each box, I wonder how heavy each book is.

Box A: total mass 12 kg

Box B: total mass 14 kg

1 **a)** How heavy is each book in Box A?

b) How heavy is each book in Box B?

What do you notice about the digits in the answer?

Share

a) 12 can be partitioned into 1 ten and 2 ones.

I will try what we did in the last lesson and divide each digit by 10.

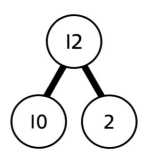

1 ten and 2 ones =
10 ones and 20 tenths

T	O	•	Tth
10	1 1	•	

10 ones ÷ 10 = 1 one

20 tenths ÷ 10 = 2 tenths

So, 12 ÷ 10 = 1 one and
        2 tenths

      = 1·2

T	O	•	Tth
	1 1 1 1 1 1 1 1 1 1 1 1	•	$\frac{1}{10}$ $\frac{1}{10}$ $\frac{1}{10}$ $\frac{1}{10}$ $\frac{1}{10}$ $\frac{1}{10}$ $\frac{1}{10}$ $\frac{1}{10}$ $\frac{1}{10}$ $\frac{1}{10}$ $\frac{1}{10}$ $\frac{1}{10}$ $\frac{1}{10}$ $\frac{1}{10}$ $\frac{1}{10}$ $\frac{1}{10}$ $\frac{1}{10}$ $\frac{1}{10}$ $\frac{1}{10}$ $\frac{1}{10}$

Each book in Box A weighs 1·2 kg.

b) We need to calculate 14 ÷ 10.

I will visualise the place value counters on a place value grid.

14 = 1 ten and 4 ones

   = 10 ones and 40 tenths

10 ones ÷ 10 = 1 one

40 tenths ÷ 10 = 4 tenths

So, 14 ÷ 10 = 1 one and 4 tenths = 1·4

Each book in Box B weighs 1·4 kg.

The digits in 14 and 1·4 are the same, but their position has changed.

Think together

1 A box of 10 identical toy cars has a mass of 23 kg.

What is the mass of each car?

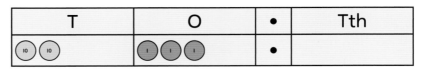

23 = 2 tens and 3 ones

= 20 ones and 30 tenths.

20 ones ÷ 10 = ☐ ones.

30 tenths ÷ 10 = ☐ tenths.

23 ÷ 10 = ☐ ones and ☐ tenths.

The mass of each toy car is ☐.☐ kg.

2 What calculation do these place value grids help you to solve?

☐ ÷ ☐ = ☐

3 What are the largest and the smallest answers for Number B that can be made in the number sentence below? Use two of the digit cards to represent Numbers A and B.

CHALLENGE

Number A ÷ 10 = Number B

| 1 | 5 | 4 |

 ÷ 10 =

Number A   Number B

I do not think using trial and error is the most efficient way to find the solutions. I will look for another way.

Is there a pattern linking the Number A values and the Number B values?

→ **Practice book 4B p132**

Hundredths

Discover

This grid is equal to one whole.

1 **a)** What fraction of the hundredths grid is covered with striped counters?

How can this be written as a decimal?

b) What fraction of the hundredths grid is covered with plain counters?

How can this be written as a decimal?

Share

a) There are 100 equal squares in the whole.

1 square is covered with a striped counter.

This can be written as $\frac{1}{100}$.

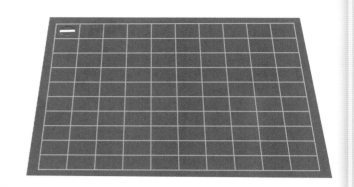

> We say this as '1 hundredth'. There is also a place value column called hundredths.

O	•	Tth	Hth
0	•	0	1

One hundredth can also be written as a decimal.

The digit 1 is placed in the hundredths column.

$\frac{1}{100}$ can be written as 0·01.

b) 10 of the 100 squares are covered by plain counters.

This can be written as $\frac{10}{100}$.

The fraction of the hundredths grid covered by plain counters is $\frac{10}{100}$.

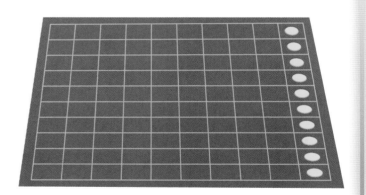

We know that 10 hundredths is equal to 1 tenth.

O	•	Tth	Hth
0	•	1	0

So $\frac{10}{100}$ can be written as a decimal as 0·10 (shows 10 hundredths) or 0·1 (shows 1 tenth).

> If I look at the columns in the hundredths grid, 1 of the 10 columns is covered with counters. I know this is written as $\frac{1}{10}$.

185

Think together

1 **a)** What fraction of the hundredths grid is covered with counters?

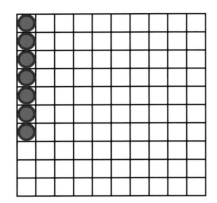

O	•	Tth	Hth
	•		

b) How could this be written as a decimal?

◻.◻◻

2 **a)** How could the decimal 0·13 be represented with counters on a hundredths grid?

b) How does each digit in 0·13 represent the counters on the grid?

The digit 1 represents

_____ .

The digit 3 represents

_____ .

3 Amelia has 11 counters to place on a hundredths grid.

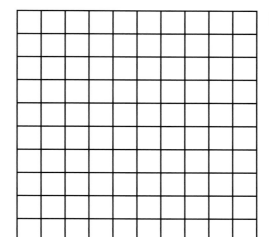

As she places each counter, she says what fraction of the hundredths grid is covered and she writes this as a decimal.

One hundredth, two hundredths, three hundredths …

0·01, 0·02, 0·03

Amelia

Complete the sequence of what she says, and what she writes.

I will place the counters in a row to help me.

What happens when I have placed 10 counters?

187

→ **Practice book 4B p135**

Hundredths ➋

Discover

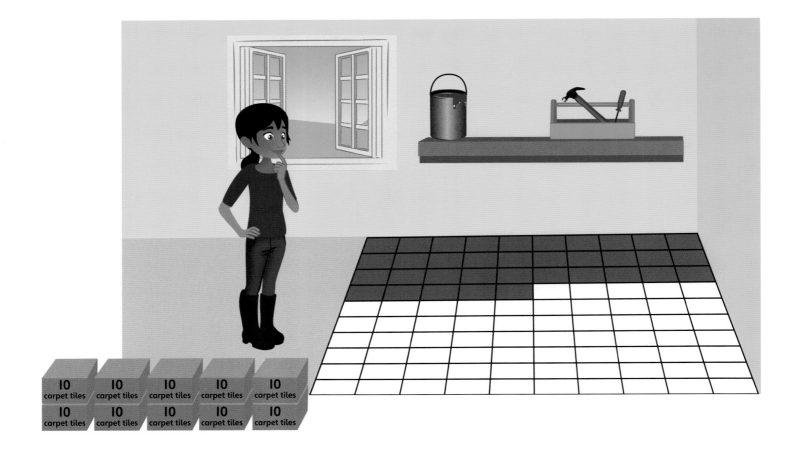

1 a) What fraction of the floor has been carpeted?

Write this as a decimal.

b) 8 more tiles are placed down. How much of the floor has been carpeted now?

Write this as a fraction and as a decimal.

Share

a) There are 100 squares altogether.

35 of the 100 squares have carpet on them.

This is $\frac{35}{100}$, or 0·35.

O	•	Tth	Hth
	•		

$\frac{35}{100}$ or 0·35 of the floor has been carpeted.

O	•	Tth	Hth
	•	$\frac{1}{10}$ $\frac{1}{10}$ $\frac{1}{10}$	$\frac{1}{100}$ $\frac{1}{100}$ $\frac{1}{100}$ $\frac{1}{100}$ $\frac{1}{100}$

> I know the 3 represents the number of complete rows of carpet tiles in the grid, and the 5 represents the other tiles.

b) 8 hundredths more than 35 hundredths is 43 hundredths.

> I will try counting on in hundredths on a number line.

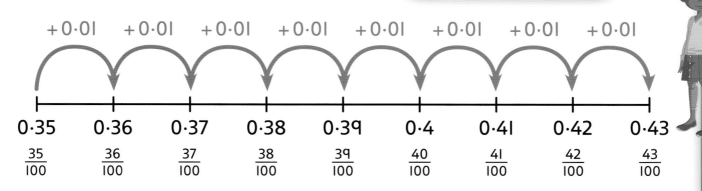

| +0·01 | +0·01 | +0·01 | +0·01 | +0·01 | +0·01 | +0·01 | +0·01 |

| 0·35 | 0·36 | 0·37 | 0·38 | 0·39 | 0·4 | 0·41 | 0·42 | 0·43 |
| $\frac{35}{100}$ | $\frac{36}{100}$ | $\frac{37}{100}$ | $\frac{38}{100}$ | $\frac{39}{100}$ | $\frac{40}{100}$ | $\frac{41}{100}$ | $\frac{42}{100}$ | $\frac{43}{100}$ |

This is $\frac{43}{100}$ or 0·43.

$\frac{43}{100}$ or 0·43 of the floor has been carpeted now.

189

Think together

1 What decimal does each of the hundredths grids show?

a)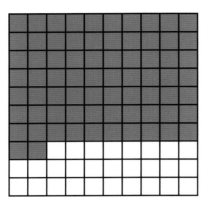

☐ squares are shaded.

This is $\dfrac{\boxed{}}{100}$ or $0 \cdot \boxed{}$.

b)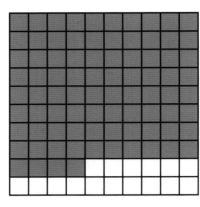

☐ squares are shaded.

This is $\dfrac{\boxed{}}{100}$ or $0 \cdot \boxed{}$.

2 In this hundredths grid, 0·21 of the whole is shaded.

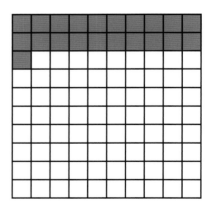

a) Tom shades 9 more squares. What fraction and decimal equivalent of the grid is shaded now?

$0 \cdot \boxed{}$, or $\dfrac{\boxed{}}{\boxed{}}$

b) How many more squares does Tom need to shade on the grid above to make $\frac{25}{100}$?

Tom needs to shade ☐ more squares.

3 Aki has 100 counters in a bag.

He drops the bag and loses some counters.

To help him to see how many counters he has lost, Aki places the ones he still has on a hundredths grid.

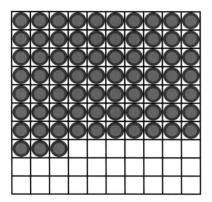

I thought that finding 70 + ☐ = 100 and 3 + ☐ = 10 would help me, but I am not sure I am right.

a) How many counters has Aki lost?

b) How can this be written as a fraction and as a decimal?

This is $\frac{☐}{100}$, or 0·☐☐

I can use my understanding of part-wholes to work out how many counters were lost.

191

→ **Practice book 4B p138**

Hundredths ③

Discover

1 a) Have Alex or Reena made 0·25?

b) What additional counters does Kate need to make 0·25?

Share

a) Reena has made 0·02 and 0·5. So Reena has made 0·52.

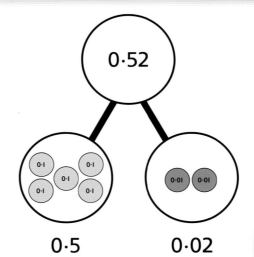

0·5   0·02

Alex has made 0·25.

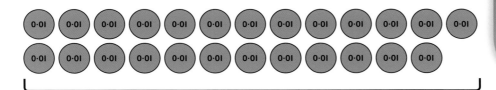

0·25

> If I count on in tenths, I know that ten 0·01 counters is the same as 0·1.

b) Kate has 2 counters that each have a value of 0·1 so Kate has 0·2.

0·25 is made up of 2 tenths and 5 hundredths.

> I will use a number line to count on from the amount Kate has made, to make the whole (0·25).

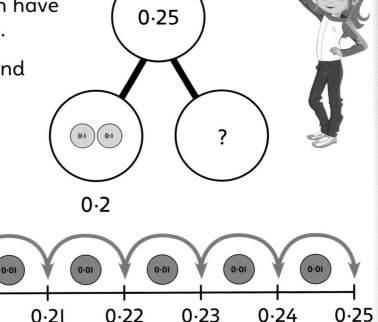

Kate needs an additional 5 hundredth counters to make 0·25.

Think together

1 Richard has the following place value counters:

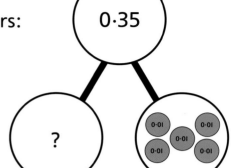

0.35

?

a) What other counters does he need to make 0·35?

Richard has ☐ 0·01 counters.

Richard needs ☐ more ☐·☐ counters.

b) Look at the number line below. How many 0·01 counters does Richard need to complete each jump?

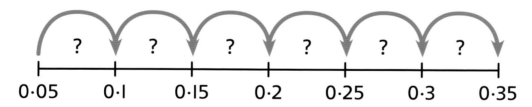

| ? | ? | ? | ? | ? | ? |

0·05   0·1   0·15   0·2   0·25   0·3   0·35

Each jump = ☐ 0·01 counters.

2 How many different ways could the decimal 0·43 be made?

☐ + ☐ = 0·43

I am going to start by using a part-whole model to separate 0·43 into tenths and hundredths.

3 How many different numbers can be made by combining two of the following groups of counters?

CHALLENGE

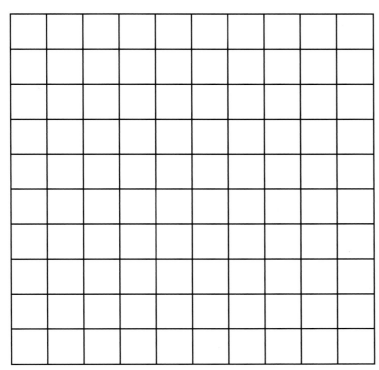

Group A

0·1 0·1 0·1

Group B

0·01 0·01 0·01

Group C

$\frac{1}{10}$ $\frac{1}{10}$
$\frac{1}{10}$ $\frac{1}{10}$

Group D

$\frac{1}{100}$ $\frac{1}{100}$
$\frac{1}{100}$ $\frac{1}{100}$

 I will start by finding all the numbers I can make by combining Group A with each of the other groups.

 I wonder if there is a quicker way than counting each counter separately.

195

→ Practice book 4B p141

Dividing by 100

Discover

1 **a)** The pizza is cut so it can be shared out to the 100 guests. How long is each piece of pizza?

b) The cake is then shared out to the 100 guests. How long is each piece of cake?

Share

a) The pizza is 3 m long.

We need to divide it into 100 pieces.

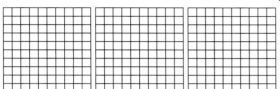

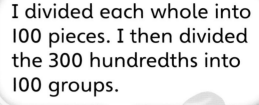

I divided each whole into 100 pieces. I then divided the 300 hundredths into 100 groups.

3 ones = 300 hundredths

300 hundredths ÷ 100 = 3 hundredths

3 ÷ 100 = 0·03 so each piece of pizza is 0·03 m long.

b) The cake is 12 m long. We need to divide this into 100 pieces too.

Method 1

12 ones = 1,200 hundredths

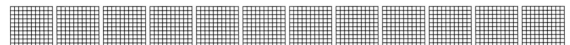

1,200 hundredths ÷ 100 = 12 hundredths

12 ÷ 100 = 0·12

So each piece of cake is 0·12 m long.

Method 2

Divide 10 of the squares into tenths and 2 of the squares into hundredths.

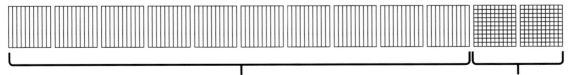

10 ones = 100 tenths	2 ones = 200 hundredths
100 tenths ÷ 100 = 1 tenth	200 hundredths ÷ 100 = 2 hundredths

1 tenth and 2 hundredths is equal to 0·12. So each piece of cake is 0·12 m long.

Think together

1 100 plates have a mass of 4 kg.

What is the mass of each plate?

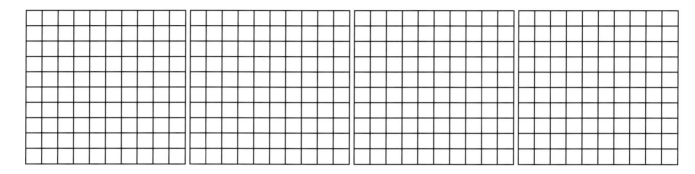

4 ones = ☐ hundredths

☐ hundredths ÷ 100 = ☐ hundredths

4 ÷ 100 = ☐.☐☐

The mass of each plate is ☐.☐☐ kg

2 **a)** A 2-digit number divided by 100 is 0·16.

What was the starting number?

☐ ÷ 100 = 0·16

b) 60 ÷ 10 = 6

How can this help us to calculate

60 ÷ 100 = ☐ ?

> To divide by 100 I know I need to divide by 10 and then divide by 10 again.

CHALLENGE

3 Three children have tried to complete different calculations.

What is the answer to Mo's calculation?

Lee

Ebo

Mo

$1 \div 100 = 0.01$

$13 \div 100 = 0.13$

$145 \div 100 = \boxed{}$

Mo's question is a new question. He should follow the same method to find the answer.

There is another way to find the solution. There is a pattern that we could use to help.

→ **Practice book 4B p144**

Dividing by 10 and 100

Discover

HAPPY BIRTHDAY

Jamilla   Richard   Max   Jamie

1 **a)** The cake must be shared equally between 10 tables of guests.
It has a mass of 32 kg.

What mass of cake would each table receive?

b) There are 100 people at the joint birthday party.

If the cake is shared equally between all of the guests, what mass
of cake would each person receive?

Share

a) The cake has a mass of 32 kg.

It must be shared equally between 10 tables. We need to work out $32 \div 10$.

32 is equal to 3 tens and 2 ones.

T	O	•	Tth
⑩ ⑩ ⑩	① ①	•	

T	O	•	Tth
	① ①	•	$\frac{1}{10}$ ×20

$32 \div 10 = 3 \cdot 2$

Each table would receive 3·2 kg of cake.

b) The cake is shared between 100 guests.

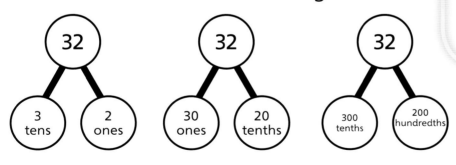

32 → 3 tens, 2 ones

32 → 30 ones, 20 tenths

32 → 300 tenths, 200 hundredths

300 tenths ÷ 100 = 3 tenths   200 hundredths ÷ 100 = 2 hundredths

3 tenths and 2 hundredths is equal to 0·32

$32 \div 100 = 0 \cdot 32$

Each person would receive 0·32 kg of cake.

I remember that I ten is equal to 10 ones and I one is equal to 10 tenths.

Remember you can write 32 as 30 ones and 20 tenths to help you divide by 10.

I exchanged until I made numbers that could divide by 100.

Think together

1 Ribbon was used to decorate each of the 100 guests' chairs. An equal length of ribbon was used for each chair. 64 m of ribbon was used altogether. What length of ribbon was used for each chair?

600 tenths ÷ 100 = ☐ tenths

400 hundredths ÷ 100 = ☐ hundredths

64 ÷ 100 = ☐ tenths and ☐ hundredths

64 m ÷ 100 = ☐.☐☐ m

Each chair is decorated with

☐.☐☐ m of ribbon.

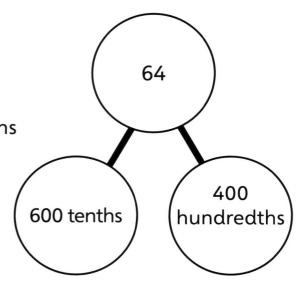

64

600 tenths

400 hundredths

2 Luis has written the following calculation. He represents his answer on a hundredths grid.

64 ÷ 100 = 0·64

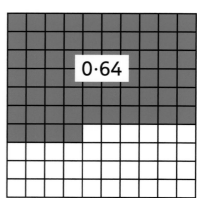

0·64

a) Is Luis's hundredths grid correct?

b) Luis says that the 6 in 0·64 represents 6 tenths. Is he correct?

3 Zac and Reena have been asked to calculate 20 ÷ 100.

Each has explained the way they calculated their answer.

I know 20 divided by 10 is 2 and that 2 divided by 10 is 0·2. So, 20 ÷ 100 = 0·2.

You cannot divide 20 by 100. 20 ones are the same as 200 tenths. 200 tenths divided by 100 is 2 tenths. 20 ÷ 100 = 0·2.

Zac

Reena

a) What is the same and what is different about the two methods used?

b) How can both methods be used to calculate 90 ÷ 100?

I wonder if there is more than one way to complete any calculation.

203

End of unit check

1 What fraction of the whole is covered with red counters?

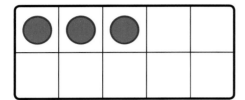

A 0·7   B 0·03   C 0·3   D 0·07

2 What is the value of the <u>underlined</u> digit?

13·1<u>9</u>

A 9 ones   C 9 hundreds

B 9 tenths   D 9 hundredths

3 Complete the following calculation:

7 ÷ 10 = ☐

A 7·0   B 7·7   C 0·7   D 0·07

4 Complete the following calculation:

24 ÷ 10 = ☐

A 20·4   B 2·4   C 0·24   D 2·04

5 Which of the following is **not** equivalent to 0·46?

A $\frac{46}{100}$

C 46 tenths

B 46 hundredths

D 3 tenths and 16 hundredths

6 Complete the calculation:

0·72 = 0·7 + ☐

A 0·2

B 0·79

C 1·42

D 0·02

7 Complete the calculation:

21 ÷ 100 = ☐

A 2·1

B 2·01

C 0·21

D 0·12

8 What number, greater than 1·6 and less than 1·7, can be made using the following digit cards?

| 6 | 1 | 7 | 0 | . |

A 1·70

B 0·61

C 1·76

D 1·67

9 Place the following numbers accurately on the number line:

1·7   1·23   1·76   1·07

```
├┼┼┼┼┼┼┼┼┼┼┼┼┼┼┼┼┼┼┼┼┼┼┼┼┼┼┼┼┼┼┼┼┼┼┼┼┼┼┼┼┼┼┼┼┼┼┼┼┼┼┼┼┼┼┤
1                                                    2
```

205

→ **Practice book 4B p150**

I shared my ideas!

I enjoyed solving these maths puzzles.

What have we learnt?

Can you do all these things?

- ⚡ Solve problems using multiplication and division
- ⚡ Count squares to find the area of a rectilinear shape
- ⚡ Identify equivalent fractions
- ⚡ Add and subtract fractions
- ⚡ Use the decimal point to show tenths and hundredths as decimals

Remember, mistakes help us learn!

Now you are ready for the next books!